Active Writing
Understand, practise, succeed

JULIA STRONG & KIM RICHARDSON

KEY STAGE 3 / YEAR 8

Contents Grid

	Section 1 – How text types work	Section 2 – Composition/effect
Imagine, explore, entertain		
A Narrative pg 6 • traditional tale • novel	R5, R7, R14, S8, R3, R10 • Ingredients of a narrative text	R14, (Wr5), (Wr7), R7, R8 • Audience and purpose • Making language choices
B Recount pg 22 • biography • autobiography	S8, R10, R3 • Audience and purpose • Using imagery and powerful language, and identifying key ideas	S9, W11, (Wr7), R10 • Ingredients of a recount text
Inform, explain, describe		
C Information pg 35 • dictionary • information book	R10, S8, R3 • Ingredients of an information text	R10, S8, S9, R5, W7c, W9, S10, S12, W12, R8 • Audience and purpose • Understanding specialist words and creating glosses
D Explanation pg 49 • information book	R10, S8, R3 • Ingredients of an explanation text	S8, R3, W11 • Considering the vocabulary, grammar and style of a text • Using figurative language
E Instruction pg 64 • radio instruction manual • notes for a secret code	R10, S8, R3 • Ingredients of an instruction text	R8, R10, S11 • Analysing and comparing two texts • Understanding Standard and non-Standard English
Persuade, argue, advise		
F Persuasion pg 78 • adverts	R13, S13e, R4, R7 • Ingredients of a persuasive text	S13e, R10, R13, R2, R14, (Wr15) • Identifying the stylistic conventions of persuade texts • Look at language choices in own writing
G Argument pg 94 • newspaper article • letters	W13, S8, R3 • Ingredients of an argument text	S9, (Wr13), (Wr14), R6 • Writing a letter on a controversial issue • Using rhetorical devices and signposting arguments • Recognising bias and sorting fact from opinion
H Advice pg 108 • campaign leaflet	(Wr15), S8, R3 • Ingredients of an advice text	S9, S12, W12 • Analysing the style and tone of advice texts
Analyse, review, comment		
I Discursive, pg 120 • discursive articles	W16, S8, R3 • Ingredients of a discursive text	(Wr16), (Wr17), R6, W11 • Considering different viewpoints • Recognising bias and sorting fact from opinion • Appreciating figurative language
J Review pg 135 • film review	(Wr18), R3 • Ingredients of a review text	(Wr18), S4, W12, W11, S12 • Considering the impact of a review • Exploring the present tense, word choice, and figurative and informal language
Exemplars section pg 147		

Section 3 – Text structure/organisation	Section 4 – Sentence structure/organisation	Section 5 – Composing own text
R3, S6 • Making notes • Exploring and using paragraphs	S1, S2, (Wr5), S3 • Using non-finite clauses • Presenting and punctuating dialogue	(Wr1), (Wr2), (Wr5), (Wr6), (Wr7) • Writing a short story, conveying character and using dialogue
R3, R10, S7 • Identifying key ideas • Linking paragraphs	S1, S2, S3 • Exploring sentence lengths and structures • Using colons and semicolons	S9, S12, (Wr2), (Wr5), (Wr12) • Writing a recount text for a particular audience
R3, R10, S6 • Using text skeletons • Grouping sentences into paragraphs	S1, S2, W10, S3 • Investigating non-finite clauses, prepositions, connectives and dashes	S9, S12, (Wr1), (Wr2), (Wr10), (Wr12) • Writing an information text, selecting appropriate material and guiding the reader
R3, R10, S6, (Wr11) • Making notes • Identifying key ideas and using linking sentences	S1, S8, S3 • Highlighting cause and effect • Using relative clauses, semicolons and other punctuation	S9, S12, (Wr1), (Wr2), (Wr11) • Writing a text explaining complex ideas
R3, R10, S6, (Wr12) • Making notes • Identifying key ideas and using linking sentences and clauses with connectives	S2, S3 • Using short, clear sentences to help the reader • Using a full range of punctuation	(Wr1), (Wr2), (Wr12) • Writing a text giving clear instructions
R7, R13, S12, R15, S8, S9, S10, S11 • Analysing writing using a text skeleton • Identifying signposts that make a text cohesive	S3, S11, R12, R14, (Wr15) • Using punctuation to show boundaries in sentences • Varying sentence length and style	(Wr1), (Wr3), (Wr15), S8, S12, S11 • Writing a persuasion text using paragraphs for cohesion and varied sentences
R10, S7, S6 • Comparing the structure of opinion letters • Grouping sentences into paragraphs	S1, S2 • Expressing complex sentences using clauses and commas • Exploring different sentence structures	(Wr1) (Wr13), (Wr14), S6, S7, S1, S2, (Wr2) • Writing a persuasive case using evidence
S9, (Wr14), (Wr15), S6 • Writing advice texts using clear signposting and taking account of possible consequences • Grouping sentences into paragraphs	S5, S9, S3 • Using conditionals and modal verbs • Writing lists coherently • Using the colon	(Wr15), (Wr14), S12, (Wr2) • Writing advice using signposts for clarity and using the correct level of formality
R3, S6, S7 • Making notes • Grouping sentences into paragraphs	S1, S2, S5, S6 • Using a variety of sentence structures and punctuation • Using tentative language	(Wr3), (Wr16), (Wr17), (Wr1), S1, S6, S7, (Wr2) • Writing a discursive essay, weighing up viewpoints and presenting a balanced analysis
R3, S6, S7 • Making notes • Using paragraphs	S2, S3, S1 • Analysing noun phrases and adjectival phrases • Punctuating using hyphens • Making complex sentences using clauses and commas	(Wr2), (Wr17), (Wr18), S2, S3, S6, S7, S4 • Writing a critical review • Exploring sentence structures, including noun phrases • Using paragraphs

W = word level, S = sentence level, R = reading, Wr = writing

Contents

Collins Active Writing 2 is a practical guide to writing in different text types for students in Year 8. It will help you increase and apply your knowledge of language, grammar and the craft of writing. *Active Writing* puts the emphasis firmly on practice through a step-by-step approach to learning the features of each text type, with every unit building towards the writing of a complete piece. This approach should enable you to tackle any type of writing task confidently.

How the book is organised

The units

The book has 10 units each focusing on one of 10 main text types that together cover all the different forms and purposes of writing. These are: Narrative, Recount, Information, Explanation, Instruction, Persuasion, Argument, Advice, Discussion and Review. The units are grouped together under the triplet headings from the National Curriculum for English.

A unit has five sections each concentrating on one aspect that makes writing effective.

Section 1 –How the text type works This gives an overview of a particular type of text, e.g. a fable in Narrative, and highlights its typical language and structural features. You will actively analyse this text using annotation and a note-making tool called a **text skeleton**.

Section 2 – Composition and effect This introduces a longer text that forms the basis of the work in Sections 2, 3, and 4. This time the focus is on the way the writer has used different language features to create specific effects. You will practise using these effects for yourself.

Section 3 – Text structure and organisation The emphasis is on the structure of the main text and how the writer has linked sections and ideas within paragraphs. Using a text skeleton and sentence frames you will analyse the structure of the main text and plan a text of your own.

Section 4 – Sentence structure and punctuation The focus is firmly on the sentence grammar and punctuation that underpins the text type. You will practise changing and developing sentences to add more variety to your writing.

Section 5 – Composing your own text This delivers the main task of the unit and is your chance to write a longer piece in the text type. As you brainstorm ideas, plan, draft and revise your own writing, you will draw on all the work you have done in Sections 1-4. To help you further, this section also provides plenty of reminders and support for the writing task.

The Exemplar section

At the back of the book are example responses for selected tasks in Sections 1 to 4. These are not intended as the 'only answer', but as a guide to how you might respond to the task. You will see ▣X when there is an exemplar for a task.

When the ▣TR icon appears next to a task, it indicates that in the Teacher's Resource there is either a black-and-white version of an example text for annotation or a worksheet to support the task.

Tasks as building blocks

The tasks in each unit provide practice in the following vital skills for writing.

- **Learning from example** – identifying text features and their effects (see page 7)
- **Planning practice** – using text skeletons to help structure writing (see page 8), thinking about audience and purpose (see page 11)
- **Spinning sentences** – understanding how to structure sentences to build up and release tension (see page 15)
- **Targeted activities** – mini-writing tasks, supported by discussion, throughout allow practice in the language features explored (see page 18) building towards the main writing task at the end of each unit (see page 20).

Part of a model answer is often provided to help students tackle a task.

The class organisation for each task is shown by the following icons:

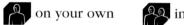 on your own  in pairs 　　 in groups

The emphasis is on interactive tasks to maximise student understanding through focused paired and group work. This builds up to support independent writing. Only the teacher introductions and class feedback and presentations are whole-class activities.

Clear explanations

Explanations of vocabulary, grammar, structure and style features are outlined through the following.

- Typical features panel – listing the form and language features of each text type – see the first page of each unit.
- Grammar panel – explaining a grammar point clearly and providing examples.
- Glossary panel – defining tricky words in texts and explanations.
- Highlighted text – emphasising each language feature consistently for instant recognition. For example, students will always know that text highlighted in orange is a topic sentence while text highlighted in mauve is a time connective (see page 147).

How *Collins Active Writing* increases confidence for the test

Students' ability to write well for a wide range of audiences and purposes is all-important in gaining a high mark in the Year 8 optional tests and end of key stage test. *Collins Active Writing* helps students prepare in several ways.

- At the start of Sections 2 and 5, Test Watch panels **Test watch** list the skills students will need to develop for the test
- The main task in Section 5 acts as full-scale practice for the type of task students will meet in the test
- On-going formative assessment is provided by the pair evaluation task 📇 and the setting of own writing targets task 🎯 at the end of Section 5. These are supported by copymasters in the Teacher's Resource
- A complete mock test with example answers related to the marking criteria is provided in the Teacher's Resource to refine students' test skills.

By using *Collins Active Writing 2* students will not only improve their writing skills and chances of success in the end of year tests, but will increase their confidence as writers.

A The Art of Narrative Writing

How narrative text works

AIMS

- Revisit the key ingredients of narrative text.
- Analyse the structure of narrative text.

In this section you will build on your existing knowledge of how a narrative text works, thinking about its audience, purpose and form, and focusing on its typical structure and language features.

Audience, purpose, form

Narrative texts tell you an imaginary story. Some typical examples are:

- **novels**, such as the *Harry Potter* series
- **traditional tales**, such as *Cinderella*
- **short stories**, such as a story you may be asked to write in an English lesson.

TYPICAL FEATURES

The typical features of narrative texts are listed below. You will need to refer to these in Section 2.

- The **audience** is someone who wants to be entertained and absorbed by a story.
- The **purpose** is to tell that story in an entertaining and interesting way. Some stories have a broader purpose, to pass on traditional culture or a moral.
- The **form** or structure of narrative often includes an opening (introduction); a series of events (the developing plot and complication); a crisis; and a resolution. Events are often narrated in chronological order and organised in chapters.

Typical **language features** of narrative texts are:

- past tense, e.g. 'was'
- in the first or third person, e.g. 'I' or 'he'
- chronological order indicated by time connectives, e.g. 'A week after'
- expressive and descriptive language, e.g. powerful verbs, nouns and adjectives, and figurative language (imagery)
- a consistent narrative perspective (how/by whom the story is told), e.g. an omniscient (all-knowing) narrator
- dialogue to develop the characters and/or plot, e.g 'And what are we to call you?'
- what characters feel, and what the narrator feels about characters, is often implied[1] rather than explicit,[2] e.g. 'Her nose twitched impatiently'.

[1] **explicit** – stated directly

[2] **implied (implicit)** – not stated directly

Reading and annotating

The first half of the story below has been annotated to show the language features listed on page 6. Annotate the second half to provide more examples of as many of the features as you can. Make a brief note of the effects they have.

Past tense

Chronological order – helps the reader understand how one event follows another

Time connective – helps reader follow the chronology of the story

This is Not an Ordinary Baby

When Nasreddin's wife died, he married again. His new wife was a widow.

A week after he married her, she had a baby.

Nasreddin at once went to the market and bought some paper, some pencils and some children's books. He came home with these things and put them beside the baby.

His wife was surprised. 'What are you doing?' she said. 'The baby won't be able to use those things for a long time. Why are you in such a hurry?'

'You are quite wrong,' answered her husband. 'Our baby is not an ordinary baby. It came in a week instead of nine months. You see, it will be ready to learn to read and write in a few weeks from now.'

Traditional tale

Third-person narrative – story told by omniscient (all-knowing) narrator

Descriptive language – rhetorical technique of repetition

Traditional tales

Traditional tales are sometimes written or told in very plain language. That is why you will have struggled to find another example of descriptive language in the story above.

The surface meaning of a traditional tale is also clear, as it is told in a straightforward way. Its underlying meaning (or message), however, isn't always immediately clear. The reader has to think about it.

Task 2 **Discussing**

Discuss the features of *This is Not an Ordinary Baby*, focusing on the following questions:

- Why is the language of traditional tales often so simple and the surface meaning so clear?
- The underlying meaning is *implied*, because it is not stated directly. Why hasn't the narrator made the message *explicit* in the story, e.g. by saying 'Nasreddin was stupid because he didn't realise...'?

Using text skeletons

In order to understand the structure of a text, it can be useful to draw a diagram or 'text skeleton'. Text skeletons represent the bare bones of a text.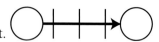

A typical narrative skeleton resembles a timeline, but remember there are many different ways to structure a story so this type of skeleton only fits the 'typical' story structure.

The lines cutting across the timeline indicate key stages in the story. The typical story has five stages, as shown below. The notes attached to each stage, e.g. 'A week later she has a baby', are memory joggers summing up the key events.

Using text skeletons will help you to analyse the structure of a text and plan your own writing.

Task 3 **Structuring**

👥 Below is a partially-completed text skeleton for *This is Not an Ordinary Baby*.
✗ Complete the text skeleton for stages 4 and 5 so that you have a full set of notes
TR on the text and a clear picture of its structure.

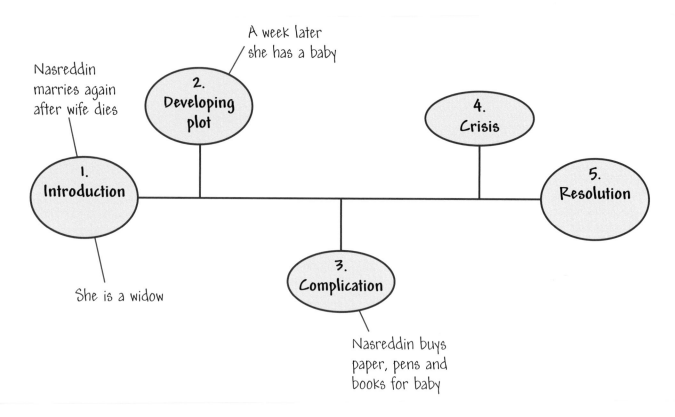

2 Composition and effect

Learning from example

AIMS

- Reinforce the key ingredients of narrative text.
- Identify how storywriters compose their writing to suit audience and purpose, using dialogue, characterisation and powerful language.
- Think about how different language choices can make meaning implicit rather than explicit.

In this section you will focus on an extract from a novel and consider how the writer has tried to engage the reader's interest.

Test watch As well as building up your writing skills, the following sections are good preparation for the optional reading tests at the end of Year 8 because they help you to:

- comment on a writer's purpose and the effects of the text on the reader
- comment on the structure and organisation of texts
- comment on a writer's use of language
- deduce, infer or interpret information, events or ideas
- describe, select or retrieve information, events or ideas from texts.

If you show these skills in the reading test, you will gain a better mark.

Task 4   Reading

In *The Wind Singer* by William Nicholson, set in Aramanth, exams are everything. Your exams determine where you live, your job, and even the colour of your clothes. Pinto Hath, called Pinpin by her family, is two years old, and today she must take her first test. Her parents and her twin brother and sister go with her.

Read the following episode from the beginning of *The Wind Singer*. As you read, consider how the author builds up the tension through the episode, and how he relieves the tension at the end.

[1] **all-embracing** – huge
[2] **instinctive** – natural

Time connectives – help reader follow chronology of story

Past tense

Expressive and descriptive language – including powerful nouns and adjectives

Third-person narrative – story told by omniscient narrator

The Wind Singer

The Examiner was <u>now</u> ready for Pinpin. He <u>approached</u> the desk, his eyes on his papers.

'Pinto Hath,' he said. And then raising his eyes, <u>his face took on an all-embracing[1] smile</u>. Pinpin met this look with instinctive[2] suspicion.

<u>'And what are we to call you, my little fellow?'</u>
<u>'By her name,' said Mrs Hath.</u>

'Well then, Pinto,' said the Examiner, still beaming. 'I've got some pretty pictures here. Let's see if you can tell me what they are.'

He presented Pinpin with a sheet of coloured images. <u>Pinpin looked, but said nothing.</u> The Examiner pointed with his finger to a dog.

Dialogue – gives insight into characters. Examiner is pompous and doesn't see that Pinpin is a girl.

[5] **Words imply** Pinpin's feelings

10

The Art of Narrative Writing

'What's this?'

Not a sound from Pinpin.

'What's this, then?'

Silence.

'Does he have a hearing problem?'

'No,' said Mrs Hath. 'She can hear you.'

'But he doesn't speak.'

'I suppose there's nothing much she wants to say.'

Bowman and Kestrel held their breath. The Examiner frowned and looked grave, and made a note on his papers. Then he returned to the pictures.

'Well now, Pinto. Show me a doggy. Where's a doggy?'

Pinpin gazed back at him, and neither spoke nor pointed.

'A house, then. Show me a little house.'

Nothing. And so it went on, until at last the Examiner put his pictures away, looking graver still.

'Let's try some counting, shall we, little chap?'

He started counting, meaning Pinpin to follow him, but all she would do was stare. He made another note.

'The last part of the test,' he said to Mrs Hath, is 'designed to assess the child's level of communication skills. Listening, understanding, and responding. We find the child is usually more at ease when held in the arms.'

'You want her in your arms?'

'If you have no objection.'

'Are you sure?'

'I have done this before, Mrs Hath. The little fellow will be quite safe with me.'

Ira Hath looked down at the ground, and her nose twitched just a little. Bowman saw this, and sent an instant thought to Kestrel.

Mama's going to crack.

But all she did was lift Pinpin from her seat and give her into the Examiner's waiting arms. Bowman and Kestrel watched with keen interest. Their father sat with his eyes closed, knowing it was all going as wrong as it possibly could, and there was nothing he could do about it. 'Well, Pinto, you're a fine fellow, aren't you?' The Examiner tickled Pinpin under the chin, and pressed her nose. 'What's this, then? Is this your nosey?'

Pinpin remained silent. The Examiner pulled out the large gold medal which hung around his neck on a chain, and dangled it in front of Pinpin's eyes. It shone in the morning light.

'Pretty, pretty. Do you want to hold it?'

Pinpin said nothing. The Examiner looked up at Mrs Hath in exasperation.[3]

'I'm not sure you realise,' he said. 'As matters stand at this moment, I shall have to give your child a zero rating.'

'Is it as bad as that?' said Mrs Hath, her eyes glittering.

'I can get nothing out of him, you see.'

'Nothing at all?'

'Is there some rhyme or word game he likes to play?'

'Let me think.' Mrs Hath proceeded, rather ostentatiously,[4] to mime

[3] **exasperation** – extreme annoyance

[4] **ostentatiously** – in an exaggerated way

the act of thinking, lips pursed,[5] finger stroking brow.

Bowman sent a thought to Kestrel.

She's cracking.

'Yes,' said Mrs Hath. 'There is a game she likes to play. Try saying to her, wiss wiss wiss.' 65

'Wiss wiss wiss?'

'She'll like that.'

Bowman and Kestrel sent the same thought at the same time.

She's cracked! 70

'Wiss wiss wiss,' said the Examiner to Pinpin. 'Wiss wiss wiss, little fellow.'

Pinpin looked at the Examiner in surprise, and wriggled a little in his arms, as if to settle herself more comfortably. Mrs Hath watched, her nose now twitching uncontrollably. Bowman and Kestrel watched, their hearts thumping. 75

Any minute now, they thought to each other.

'Wiss wiss wiss,' said the Examiner.

'Any minute now,' said Mrs Hath.

Now, Pinpin, now, willed Bowman and Kestrel. *Do it now.*

Mr Hath opened his eyes and saw the looks on their faces. Suddenly 80 realising what was going on, he rose from the bench and reached out his arms.

'Let me take her –'

Too late.

Hubba hubba Pinpin! exulted[6] Bo and Kess in the joyous silence of their 85 thoughts. *Hubba hubba Pinpin*!

A faraway look of contentment on her round face, Pinpin was emptying her bladder in a long and steady stream down the Examiner's arms. The Examiner felt the spread of the gentle warmth without at first understanding what was happening. 90

Then seeing the look of rapt[7] attention on the faces of Mrs Hath and her children, he dropped his gaze downward. The stain was seeping into his scarlet cloak. In utter silence, he held Pinpin out for Mr Hath to take, and turned and walked gravely back up the aisle.

[5] **pursed** – forming a small 'O' shape

[6] **exulted** – rejoiced

[7] **rapt** – absorbed, spellbound

Audience, purpose and content

Task 5 **Discussing**

Every writer has to start by thinking about audience and purpose. Discuss who and what you think the audience and purpose of *The Wind Singer* extract is.

Then discuss the content of the extract:

- What are the three tests that Pinpin has to take?
- How do we know that the experience is becoming too much for Mrs Hath by line 41?
- What is the decision that Mrs Hath takes at line 63? How does the writer imply that something dreadful is going to happen?
- Explain what happens in the final section of the extract.

Features of narrative text

Like all other types of writing, good narrative depends on selecting the right ingredients and combining them effectively. The opening of this extract has been annotated to bring out some key ingredients (see the Typical Features panel, page 6).

Task 6 — Annotating

Annotate the next section of the extract (up to line 29, 'He made another note') to illustrate one more example of each of these features and their effects.

Effective dialogue

Dialogue is a very common feature of narrative (it forms over half of *The Wind Singer* extract). If dialogue is handled well, it can:

- move the plot forward
- give us insight into the characters
- provide a balance to descriptive writing, or simple narrative.

Task 7 — Discussing

Discuss the use of dialogue in this extract, focusing on the following questions:

- There are six characters in the extract and yet almost all the dialogue is between Mrs Hath and the Examiner. Why do you think the author has done this?
- Bowman and Ketrel send their thoughts to each other. How does the writer make this look like dialogue? What is different about it? Is it effective?
- Even though Pinpin says nothing, she has her own 'dialogue' with the Examiner. How does the writer bring this out?

Effective characters

The success of a narrative depends on creating believable characters who are different from each other and immediately interesting. So how does William Nicholson make the characters in this extract different and interesting? One thing he does *not* do is to make the qualities of their characters explicit. If Nicholson had wanted to be *explicit*, he might have written: 'The Examiner was a pompous man with no real understanding of what others were feeling.' Instead he makes their qualities *implicit*:

- by describing what they say or do
- by showing how other characters react to them.

For example, the description in lines 3–4 ('his face took on an all-embracing smile') shows that the smile is both overdone and not really genuine.

Task 8 — Analysing characters

In groups of three, draw up a grid like the one started below to analyse how the author builds up his characters. Split the characters between you, as shown:

- Student 1 – Mrs Hath and Mr Hath
- Student 2 – the Examiner and Pinpin/Pinto
- Student 3 – Kestrel and Bowman

Character	Evidence • **What they say** • **What they do** • **How others react**	What this says about the character
The Examiner	Is given no name – just 'the Examiner' (line 1, etc.) 'And what are we to call you, my little fellow?' (line 5)	He is a distant, unfriendly person. He is pompous and doesn't notice that Pinpin is a girl.
Mrs Hath	'By her name' (line 6)	Short response is almost rude – she is angry, but can't be open about it.
Pinpin		

Effective language

The author's use of language is quite restrained or controlled in the first half of the extract, and the characters' feelings are mostly hidden.

However, effective descriptive language is also used, particularly at the end. For example, 'Bowman and Kestrel watched, their hearts thumping' is much more effective than 'Bowman and Kestrel watched. They were very nervous.' This concrete description showing what is happening to them is more powerful than simply telling us what they are feeling.

Task 9 — Writing

Rewrite the following sentences to make them more effective. Focus on replacing the underlined text with a vivid phrase or description, as in the Kestrel and Bowman example above. You may need to alter the structure of the sentence(s), as in the example:

1. <u>She felt very sad</u> because her birthday was over.
   Tears welled up in her eyes because she thought her birthday was over.

2. <u>He couldn't understand it</u>. His keys were there a moment ago.

3. Jack still hadn't done his homework, and <u>his dad was furious</u>.

4. <u>Hannah was still fast asleep</u> when the alarm went off again.

Text structure and organisation

Getting the structure right

AIMS

- Use a text skeleton to make notes on a text.

- Explore how paragraphing and other methods help to build up tension.

In this section you will use a text skeleton to help analyse the structure of the episode from *The Wind Singer* and think about what helps to build up tension in the extract.

Structuring the story

Even though *The Wind Singer* extract is not a complete story, it shows how well-crafted episodes often begin with an introduction, develop the plot and lead to a crisis, which is resolved. This is the same shape as the narrative skeleton, explored in Section 1 on page 8.

Task 10 — Analysing and discussing

Below is a partially-completed text skeleton for the extract. Complete it by adding three or four memory joggers each for stages 4 and 5 so that you have a full set of notes on the text and a clear picture of its structure.

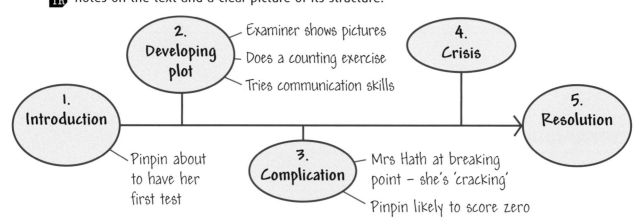

Task 11 — Discussing

When Pinpin empties her bladder on the Examiner, this resolves the crisis of 'What is going to happen?' But it also sets up another crisis – 'How is the Examiner going to respond?' The author only implies the answer to this second question.

Discuss what would be the most effective resolution of this episode and make a note of your ideas. For example:

- The Examiner announces that Pinpin has failed, and outlines the consequences for her family.
- Mr Hath's gloomy thoughts on how Pinpin's failure will badly affect the family's fortunes.
- There is another scenario that ends the chapter effectively.
- There is no resolution – the chapter ends here.

Be prepared to present your ideas.

The Art of Narrative Writing

Using structure to build up tension

The way in which you structure a narrative can help to build up the tension. In this passage, the author uses two structural features – paragraph length and the repeated pattern of Bowman and Kestrel's thoughts – to build up and release the tension.

Task 12 **Analysing**

The twins Bowman and Kestrel send thoughts to each other about what is going on (the sentences in italics).

Add a vertical jagged line ⋎ to your narrative skeleton (from Task 10) to mark where each thought occurs. Do you notice a particular pattern in their use? How effective is this technique?

The length of each paragraph in the Crisis (roughly lines 63–84) is much shorter than in the Resolution (roughly lines 85–94). Discuss what effect this has. How does it reflect what is going on in the narrative in terms of pace and tension?

Task 13 **Planning practice**

Think of an embarrassing incident that might happen to someone who is taking a test or doing something in public. Take turns to narrate the incident briefly to each other.

Discuss how you could build up the tension in the story. For example, is the audience kept in the dark about what might happen, or whether it will happen? Can you introduce a repeated thought or phrase to add impact, like Kestrel and Bowman's 'She's going to crack'…'She's cracked'?

Then use a narrative text skeleton to plan the outline for the story. Mark where any repeated thought or phrase may occur, as you did on the skeleton for *The Wind Singer*. Adapt one of the examples below if you are stuck.

- You are playing the lead part in the school play, but you can feel the elastic in your trousers breaking. Repeated phrase: *Only ten/five/two minutes to go* or *What was that noise?*
- You are in school assembly, which you know will end with two minutes' silence out of respect for a famous person who has just died. You can feel a sneezing fit coming on. Repeated phrase: *Here it comes again.*

Sentence structure and punctuation

Making the sentences work

AIMS

- Vary commentary and sentence structure by using non-finite clauses.

- Explore different methods of presenting dialogue to make it clear but varied, as well as correctly punctuated.

In this section you will develop your ability to improve your writing by varying your sentence structure. You will focus on dialogue and on using clauses beginning with '-ing' verbs.

Using non-finite clauses

GRAMMAR

Non-finite clauses are those clauses beginning with infinitives or participles (**verb phrases**) which cannot form sentences on their own, for example:

Infinitive ———— • _To smile_ broadly

Present participle ———— • _Smiling_ broadly

Past participle ———— • _Having smiled_ broadly

Non-finite clauses beginning with the present participle (the verb + 'ing', e.g. smiling, walking, speaking) allow you to link two things that are happening at the same time, without using 'and', for example:

Non-finite clause — _Smiling broadly, he approached the desk._ —— Main clause

---

Task 14 **Discussing**

 Read the sentences below from _The Wind Singer_ and compare them with the similar sentences. Discuss which set of sentences is more effective, and why.

From _The Wind Singer_	Similar sentences
He started counting, <u>meaning Pinpin to follow him</u>, but all she would do was stare.	He started counting, and meant Pinpin to follow him, but all she would do was stare.
Their father sat with his eyes closed, <u>knowing it was all going as wrong as it possibly could</u>.	Their father sat with his eyes closed. He knew it was all going as wrong as it possibly could.
<u>Suddenly realising what was going on</u>, he rose from the bench and reached out his arms.	Suddenly he realised what was going on, and rose from the bench and reached out his arms.

Note: The underlined clauses are the **non-finite clauses**. They are useful if you want to vary the structure of your sentences so that you don't have a string of clauses beginning 'and' or 'but'.

The Art of Narrative Writing

Writing

Rewrite the sentences below so that they include a non-finite clause. Remember to mark the end of the clause with a comma. You may need to change the order of the words.

1. She scratched her nose and sniffed but made no reply.

2. He threw up his arms in horror and said, 'I don't believe it!'

3. Paula entered the kitchen. She was greeted with a gruesome sight.

4. The motorbike overtook the lorry on a bend and skidded into the ditch.

Presenting dialogue

In lengthy passages of dialogue, it is important to make it clear who is speaking. However, repeating 'he said' and 'she said' can be very dull. Good writers, therefore, try to structure the dialogue in a variety of ways.

William Nicholson uses these methods in the extract from *The Wind Singer* on pages 9–11.

A Giving the full name of the speaker, e.g.
'Any minute now,' said Mrs Hath. (line 78)

B Using a pronoun ('he' or 'she') instead of the name, e.g.
'The last part of the test,' he said… (line 30)

C Naming the speaker in a separate sentence before or after the speech, e.g.
'Well, Pinto, you're a fine fellow, aren't you?' The Examiner tickled Pinpin under the chin. (lines 45–46)

D Leaving out the name of the speaker altogether, e.g.
'What's this, then?' (line 13).

E Interrupting the speech with 'he or she said', e.g.
'No,' said Mrs Hath. 'She can hear you.' (line 16)

Top tip These methods can be combined with using different 'speaking' verbs instead of 'said', e.g. 'replied', 'objected' or 'whispered'. These words should not be overused, however, as they can drown out what is actually being said.

Task 16 **Analysing**

Read lines 25 to 63 of the extract on pages 10–11 and note down how often the author has used the different ways of presenting dialogue listed in A to E above. Then answer these questions:

• Is the dialogue in this section clear? Do we know who is speaking? How?

• How many different styles of dialogue does he use?

• How effective is it overall?

The Art of Narrative Writing

3 Planning the structure

Using the improvisations or brainstormed ideas you have just seen, sketch a narrative skeleton to help you plan your story outline, adapting it as necessary.

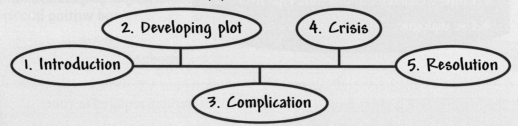

2. Developing plot

4. Crisis

1. Introduction

5. Resolution

3. Complication

4 Discussing what you're going to write

Take it in turns to present your story outline to your partner. When you are not presenting, listen carefully and be prepared to offer advice on how to develop or add detail to the storyline.

Your role is to make suggestions to help your partner. Adapt your plan, if appropriate, in the light of this discussion.

5 Composing your piece

Now you are ready to start writing.

Points to remember

As you write, remember to:

- make your narrative perspective consistent, e.g. write from the perspective of the schoolchild or the examiner, or the omniscient narrator
- use chronological order and time connectives to make your story easy to follow
- build up tension, e.g. by keeping information from the reader; by repeating a phrase/sentence; or by making your sentences/paragraphs shorter at the end (see page 15)
- select powerful vocabulary that will entertain the reader and help them picture the scene (see page 13)

- select the right amount of speech to help tell your story and reveal character, and use a variety of methods to structure this dialogue (see page 12)
- check that the speech is correctly punctuated (see page 18)
- use the speech and actions of the characters to imply what kind of people they are, rather than stating it explicitly (see page 12)
- vary the structure of your sentences, for example by including non-finite clauses (see pages 16–17)
- sustain some verb tenses.

You may want to use some of the sentence signposts and repeated phrases below to help you.

Sentence signposts and repeated phrases
- The day I was to take my piano exam *(first person – child's viewpoint)*
- When X came to the front of the class, I *(first person – examiner's/teacher's viewpoint)*
- When X came to the front of the class, Mr Y *(third person – omniscient narrator)*
- *It's going to get out, I thought.*
- *Will he recognise me?*
- *Just wait till I get home.*

6 Peer comment

Swap your draft with your partner's and read each other's carefully. Using the list on page 20, discuss what works well and highlight this on the draft. Then discuss how you could improve particular sections. Jot down your suggestions on the draft.

Redraft your writing where necessary, using your partner's comments to guide you.

7 Pulling it all together

Listen to extracts from stories written by members of your class.

Decide what are the key features that make these extracts effective. Be prepared to feed your ideas back to the class.

Set up to three targets for yourself for improving your next piece of narrative writing.

B The Art of Recount Writing

How recount text works

AIMS

- Revisit the key ingredients of recount text.
- Use a text skeleton to analyse the structure of recount text.

In this section you will build on your existing knowledge of how a recount text works, thinking about its audience, purpose and form, and focusing on its typical structure and language features.

Audience, purpose and form

Recount texts retell a series of events that have actually happened. Some typical examples are:

- **diary entries**, in which someone records what happened to them on that day
- **biographies/autobiographies**, which tell someone else's or own life story
- **newspaper articles** that recount an incident
- **sections of a history text**.

At school you will read and write recount texts, particularly in English and History. The main feature that distinguishes a recount text from a narrative (see page 6) is that the events described are true.

TYPICAL FEATURES

The typical features of recount texts are listed below. You will need to refer to these in Section 2.

- The **audience** is someone who is interested in what happened.
- Its **purpose** is to tell that person what happened clearly, or in an entertaining way.
- The **form** or structure is a description of a series of events. It may include a chronological sequence, starting at the beginning and ending at the end; time connectives to reinforce the chronological structure, e.g. 'then' or 'next'; paragraphs that mark a change of focus, time or place; and topic sentences which help to structure text by highlighting the key focus of a paragraph.

Typical **language features** of recount texts are:

- past tense, e.g. 'They went'
- third person (first person if autobiography), e.g. 'He remembered' ('I remembered')
- time connectives, e.g. 'Then one day'
- specific dates/times/names of people/places
- descriptive language to bring the events alive, e.g. use of adjectives, adverbs, powerful verbs and imagery.[1]

[1] **imagery** – the use of language to create a vivid image or picture. Metaphors and similes are common forms of imagery.

Reading and annotating

The following extract is from a biography of Louis Braille. The first half has been annotated to illustrate some of the language features of a recount text. Read the text and annotations carefully. Annotate the second half to show more examples of these ingredients and comment on their effects.

Time connective and specific date – makes chronology clear

Third person

Past tense

New paragraph – marks a change in focus by returning to other pupils

Powerful adjective – for description

Specific name – the focus is on an individual

Paragraphs – organised in chronological order

The Dawn of Braille[1]

By October, when the new school year began, Louis felt his alphabet was ready. He had found a way of forming all the letters of the alphabet, the accents, punctuation marks and mathematical signs using just six dots and some small horizontal dashes.

The other pupils, when they heard, could not contain their excitement. They gathered around in groups as Louis wrote with dazzling speed and accuracy. Within hours the whole school knew, and Louis was summoned to Dr Pignier to show what he had done.

The Director watched the rapid demonstration with fascination: it was so simple, so accurate, and so clear. Just six dots: but the brilliant child had found a way of forming them into sixty-three combinations. The Director congratulated the young pupil and urged him to continue his experiments.

For blind people, it was, unquestionably, the dawn of a new age.

[1] **braille** – the system of raised-point reading and writing used by blind people. It was invented by Louis Braille in 1824 while he was still a schoolboy.

Topic sentences

Topic sentences are used to introduce the key focus of each paragraph. They are often the first sentence of a paragraph. If you summarise the topic sentences, you get a picture of the whole passage.

 Task 2 **Summarising**

Complete the summary below by adding the key focus of the last two paragraphs of the extract.

Why do you think the final paragraph has only one sentence?

Paragraph 1: Louis' alphabet ready

Paragraph 2: Other pupils in school excited

Paragraph 3:

Paragraph 4:

The Art of Recount Writing

Using text skeletons

In order to understand the structure of a text, it can be useful to draw a diagram or 'text skeleton'. Text skeletons represent the bare bones of the text.

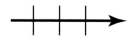

The typical recount skeleton, showing how one thing leads to another, is given below. It looks like a timeline, with the key events shown by the vertical lines. Notes summarising these events, such as 'Louis' alphabet system is ready', are called memory joggers because they help you remember the important details. An introduction or a concluding summary of the whole piece are shown by a circle at either end.

Using text skeletons will help you to analyse the structure and content of a text, and plan your own writing.

Task 3 **Structuring**

Below is a partially-completed text skeleton for *The Dawn of Braille*. Discuss and note down the memory joggers you would add for the remaining stages of the skeleton.

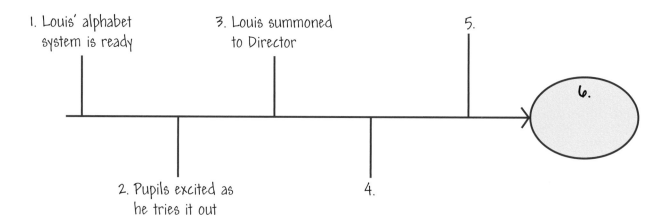

Share your skeleton with that of another pair. Have you chosen the same events to include on it?

Mark the paragraph breaks on the text skeleton with short double lines like this //. How do they relate to the main events, if at all?

Learning from example

AIMS

- Identify how a writer adapts the stylistic conventions of recount text to suit audience and purpose.

- Comment on how writers use imagery and powerful language to engage the reader's interest.

- Identify how key ideas are developed through a text.

In this section you will focus on the techniques one writer has used to try to engage the reader's interest in a recount text about learning to read.

Test watch As well as building up your writing skills, the following sections are good preparation for the optional reading tests at the end of Year 8 because they help you:

- comment on a writer's purpose and the effects of the text on the reader

- comment on the structure and organisation of texts

- comment on a writers' use of language

- deduce, infer or interpret information, events or ideas

- describe, select or retrieve information, events or ideas from texts.

If you show these skills in the reading test, you will gain a better mark.

A personal history

Task 4 **Reading and discussing**

 On page 26 is part of the introductory chapter of Alberto Manguel's *A History of Reading*. This book is an account, written for adults, of people's fascination with books and the written word from ancient times to the present day. Discuss these questions.

- What is its audience and purpose?
- Why has Alberto Manguel begun this history in such a personal way?
- How effective is his language and style in recounting his breakthrough into reading?

The Art of Recount Writing

First person – autobiographical passage

Descriptive language – boy described in great detail for effect

Connective – reinforces structure of paragraph

Past tense

Use of imagery and powerful language – engages reader's interest

5I first discovered that I could read at the age of four. I had seen, over and over again, the letters that I knew (because I had been told) were the names of the pictures under which they sat. The boy drawn in thin black lines, dressed in red shorts and a green shirt, was also somehow, I realized, the stern black shapes beneath him, as if the boy's body had been chopped up into three clean-cut figures: one arm and the *torso*,[1] **b**; the severed head so perfectly round, **o**; and the limp, low-hanging legs, **y**. I drew eyes in the round face, and a smile, and filled in the hollow circle of the torso. But there was more: I knew that not only did these shapes mirror the boy above them, but they also could tell me precisely what the boy was doing, arms stretched out and legs apart. **The boy runs**, said the shapes. He wasn't jumping, as I might have thought, or pretending to be frozen into place, or playing a game whose rules and purpose were unknown to me. **The boy runs**.

the boy runs

And yet *these realizations were common acts of conjuring*,[2] less interesting because someone else had performed them for me. Another reader – my nurse, probably – had explained the shapes and now, every time the pages opened to the image of this high-spirited boy, I knew what the shapes beneath him meant. There was pleasure in this, but it wore thin. There was no surprise.

Then one day, from the window of a car (the destination of that journey is now forgotten), I saw a billboard[3] by the side of the road. The sight could not have lasted very long; perhaps the car stopped for a moment, perhaps it just slowed down long enough for me to see, large and looming, shapes similar to those in my book, but shapes that I had never seen before.

And yet, all of a sudden, I knew what they were; I heard them in my head, they metamorphosed[4] from black lines and white spaces into a solid, sound-filled, meaningful reality. I had done this all by myself. No one had performed the magic for me. I and the shapes were alone together, revealing ourselves in a silently respectful dialogue. Since I could turn bare lines into a living reality, I was all-powerful. I could read.

5

10

15

20

25

30

35

[1] **torso** – the human body without the head, arms and legs

[2] **these realizations were common acts of conjuring** – this knowledge was like a simple magic trick

[3] **billboard** – large advertising poster

[4] **metamorphosed** – changed shape

Summarising the content

The best way of considering what a text is about is to look at the topic sentences. The first two topic sentences have been highlighted in orange in the extract.

Task 5   Topic sentences

Identify the remaining topic sentences, and be prepared to use these sentences to summarise the extract.

Features of recount text

The first part of the extract has been annotated to bring out some key features of recount text (see the Typical Features panel on page 22). Note that the first person has been used in this passage because it is autobiographical.

Task 6   Annotating

Annotate the rest of the text to illustrate other examples of as many of these features as possible.

Writing powerful prose

Many recount texts do far more than simply relate a series of events in a clear and straightforward way. These texts – including *A History of Reading* – try to engage and entertain the reader through the way in which they tell the story.

Two of the ways in which Alberto Manguel does this are by:

- using **powerful nouns**, **verbs and adjectives** in his descriptions, e.g. 'the stern black shapes' and 'They metamorphosed'
- using **imagery** to help the reader 'see' what is happening, e.g. the shapes of the letters in 'boy' are compared to different body shapes.

Task 7   Discussing and recording

Reread aloud the extract from *A History of Reading*. Identify where the writer has used powerful language and imagery, and discuss how effective this is. Make a note of your findings in a table like the one below.

Powerful language/imagery	Effect
'I discovered'	More powerful than 'I learned to read' – suggests suddenness and wonder
'stern black shapes'	Emphasises that learning to read is difficult and not v. enjoyable. Contrast with colourful picture of boy?
'as if the boy's body had been chopped up'	
'the severed head so perfectly round'	

Be prepared to present your conclusions.

Getting the structure right

AIMS

- Use a text skeleton to analyse the structure of a recount text.

- Analyse the overall structure of a text to identify how key ideas are developed.

- Identify effective ways of linking paragraphs.

In this section you will first analyse the structure of the extract from *A History of Reading* using a skeleton. Then you will explore how the text hangs together, focusing on how paragraphs look both forwards and back across the text.

Creating a text skeleton

Text skeletons sum up the structure of a text in a visual way (see page 24). The skeleton for a recount text will help you understand the structure of the extract from *A History of Reading* on page 26.

Task 8 Structuring

Look at the text skeleton for the beginning of the passage below. Complete the skeleton for the rest of the passage.

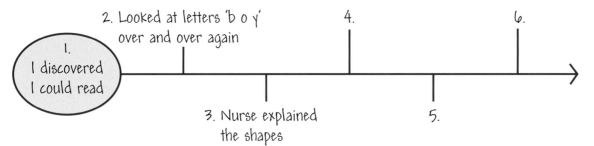

Setting the scene

The first sentence of the passage ('I first discovered that I could read at the age of four') is not the first event of the recount, but a summary of what the whole passage is about. That is why it is placed in the circle at the beginning of the timeline.

Task 9 Discussing

Discuss the following questions.

- What is the effect of the writer telling his readers right at the beginning what the passage is about?
- The main verb in the second sentence is 'had seen'. Why has the author used this tense rather than just using 'seen'?
- Why does the writer return to the statement 'I could read' at the end of the passage?

Be prepared to share your conclusions.

Paragraphs looking both ways

New paragraphs are often used to show that there is a new focus in the writing, for example when a different idea is explored. However, a new paragraph also needs to be linked to the previous paragraph or the movement of ideas will not be clear to the reader.

Each paragraph, then, needs to 'look' both ways:

New paragraph connects with the previous one – here, the connective tells you that the previous paragraph was last year

New paragraph, beginning: 'The following year...'

New paragraph focuses on a new point/time/place – here, the connective tells you that the new paragraph deals with events a year later

The best way of showing how one paragraph (or sentence) connects with those on either side is to signal this fact with a connective (see page 128).

Two common types of connective are:

- **connectives of time**, e.g. 'Later', 'Finally', 'After six hours'
- **connectives of opposition**, e.g. 'Nevertheless', 'However', 'On the contrary'.

Task 10 | Discussing

Look at the way in which Manguel has used paragraphing in the extract from his book.

- What new focus does each paragraph give?
- How is it connected to the paragraph before?

Task 11 | Planning practice

One person should recount how they spent the weekend, while their partner makes notes of the key points.

Construct a timeline of your partner's weekend, indicating what happened when.

Sat 9am breakfast

10am football practice

Use this timeline to plan a recount entitled 'Your Weekend: A Short History'. Sketch out a recount skeleton and memory joggers, basing it on your timeline. Decide where you are going to make the paragraph breaks – will they go after each main block of time, or after each significant event? Indicate these as parallel lines (//) across the skeleton.

Finally, describe the focus of each paragraph and provide a possible opening sentence for each one (including a connective where appropriate).

Sentence structure and punctuation

Making the sentences work

AIMS

- Explore the impact of using a variety of sentence lengths and structures.

- Make good use of a range of punctuation, especially the colon and semicolon.

In this section you will investigate how to use different types of sentence and punctuation to create more appealing and interesting writing.

Making complex sentences

Alberto Manguel combines short sentences with long, elegant sentences to create the effect that he wants in this passage. Longer sentences are often complex sentences. For example:

'I had seen, over and over again, the letters that I knew (because I had been told) were the names of the pictures under which they sat.'

Compare this with the three short sentences that he could have used instead:

'I had seen the same letters over and over again. They were the names of the pictures under which they sat. I knew this because I had been told it.'

The second version sounds dull in comparison. It also does not make the connection between the sentences clear. It is also not as elegant in style.

Task 12 | **Structuring** ━━━━━━━━━━━━━

 Practise writing complex sentences to make your recounts more interesting and effective. Change each of the pairs (or triplets) of short sentences below into a complex sentence by using subordinate clauses.

You will need to use subordinating conjunctions to introduce these clauses, such as 'when', 'although', 'if', 'since', 'as', 'because', 'so that', or use relative clauses. Note: You can combine these sentences in different ways; you may need to alter the wording.

1. Tom is always late for school. His teacher has decided to take action.
   <u>Since</u> *Tom is always late for school, his teacher has decided to take action.*

2. This book on the Egyptians is interesting. I found it in the library.

3. They went on arguing. The neighbours banged on the wall.

4. Susan felt hungry. As usual, she found herself in the kitchen. She raided the fridge.

5. The clock struck twelve. There was a knock at the door. It woke everyone up.

GRAMMAR

A **complex sentence** is a sentence with one or more subordinate clauses.

A **subordinating conjunction** is a word or phrase that introduces a subordinate clause, e.g. 'when' or 'although'.

A **relative clause** is a particular kind of subordinate clause which adds information to the main clause by using the pronouns 'who, 'which', 'that', etc.

Varying sentence length

A piece of writing in which the sentences are all the same length is in danger of sending its readers to sleep. One way of engaging the reader, therefore, is to vary the length of your sentences.

 Task 13 **Analysing**

Annotate the extract from *A History of Reading* to analyse the lengths of the sentences and their effect. You could divide them into three categories: *short* (less than one line), *medium* (1–2 lines) and *long* (more than 2 lines). Then discuss:

- How many sentences are there in each category?
- Does any pattern emerge? If so, what is it?
- There are several shorter sentences at the end of the passage. What effect does this have?
- What effect does the variety of sentence length have overall in the passage?

Colons and semicolons

 Task 14 **Discussing**

Another way in which Alberto Manguel has made his sentences more varied and interesting is by using colons and semicolons to add clauses. Scan the extract from *A History of Reading* on page 26 and identify any colons and semicolons. Read the grammar panel below and discuss these questions.

- What purpose does each colon have in *A History of Reading*?
- What purpose does each semicolon have?

Be prepared to share your conclusions.

GRAMMAR

The **colon** is a punctuation mark with three main uses:

1. To introduce a list, e.g. 'You will need these tools: a hammer, six nails, some string and a wooden baton.'

2. To introduce an example or quotation, e.g. 'This was the message: "Phone soon".'

3. To introduce a second clause that expands on, explains or illustrates the first, e.g. 'He ought to look happy: he's just won the lottery.'

In general, the colon points the reader's attention forward and introduces something, as if to say 'as follows'.

The **semicolon** has two main uses:

1. To separate lengthy items in a list, e.g. 'You will need these tools: a heavy hammer; six 3-inch nails; a length of string; and a wooden baton.'

2. To separate two clauses, each of which could stand on its own, e.g. 'He's a very successful businessman; he's also just won the lottery.'

AIMS

- Plan, draft and present a text describing an event in detail and in an entertaining way.
- Adapt the conventions and formality of recount text to fit a particular audience and purpose.
- Re-read and revise the work to anticipate the effect on the reader.

Your task

In this section you will compose a piece recounting your own early experiences of reading.

Test watch This writing task is good preparation for the type of writing required in your English tests because it helps you learn how to:

- plan your work so that it is organised logically into well-constructed paragraphs that are coherently linked together
- compose your writing effectively to match its audience and purpose,

- selecting appropriate vocabulary
- structure your sentences appropriately and punctuate them correctly.

If you show these skills in the optional English test at the end of Year 8, you will gain a better mark.

1 Audience and purpose

You have been asked to take part in a survey on early reading experiences. Your task is to write a memoir[1] of your own early reading. Your memories could relate to any kind of reading matter, whether it is books, magazines, comics – or even cereal packets! Your audience will be adults and other young people who like reading, and who like reading about other people's experiences.

[1] **memoir** – a piece of writing about your life or experiences

2 Discuss

Discuss what effect the audience and purpose of this task will have on the style. In particular, consider these questions.

- Will this be a clear and straightforward

recount of a series of events, or something more descriptive?
- How formal should the language be?
- How much detail is appropriate?

3 Brainstorming the content

Brainstorm all the kinds of text that you read when you were young. Which experiences have stayed with you? Were there particular books, passages, articles or illustrations that you can never forget? Or a particular place where you

read, or person who read to you?

Share your experiences of how or when you read these books and what made them special. Note down details about particular books, memories or events linked to them.

Planning the form and structure

 Select two or three incidents or features of your own history of reading, and construct a timeline so that you deal with them in chronological order. Will you give each reading experience a single paragraph, or focus on one book or event in more detail? Mark where you are going to divide the paragraphs on your timeline using the new-paragraph symbol //.

Think about an introduction to set the scene. Make a note of this, and add it to the front of the timeline. Bear in mind also that you will need to round the piece off in a satisfying way. You may want to pick up an idea, an image or a phrase from your introduction and add it to your 'Conclusion' in a circle at the end of your timeline.

 Discussing what you are going to write

 Take it in turns to present your memoir plan to your partner. When you are not presenting, listen carefully and be prepared to offer advice on how to develop or add detail to the memoir.

Your role is to make suggestions to help your partner. Adapt your plan, if appropriate, in the light of this discussion.

Composing your piece

Now you can start drafting your memoir.

Points to remember

As you write, remember to:

- use topic sentences early in each paragraph to make it clear what you are writing about (see page 23)
- provide some detailed descriptions, including powerful verbs and adjectives (see page 27)
- use imagery to help the reader 'see' what you are describing (see page 27)
- make your paragraphs connect with what has gone before, using different connectives of time and opposition, as well as focus on a new point or time (see page 29)
- include some long sentences by using subordinate clauses (see page 30)
- vary your sentence length to keep the reader's interest (see page 31)
- use colons and semicolons accurately, where appropriate (see page 31).

You may want to use some of the sentence signposts and connectives below to help you.

> ### Sentence signposts and connectives
> - When I think about what I read as a young child
> - The word 'reading' is too dull in itself to describe
> - My very earliest memory
> - But this was only the first of many
> - When I was x years old
> - I wasn't really into reading until
> - I can still hear my mother's/teacher's voice reading
> - I always pictured myself
> - However
> - And yet
> - Above all
> - Looking back, then

7 Peer comment

 Swap your draft with your partner's and read each other's carefully. Discuss what he or she needs to do to improve their recount and make it appropriate for the audience and purpose. Note up to three suggestions on the draft.

Redraft the selected sections of your memoir using the comments to guide you.

8 Pulling it all together

  Listen to some of the memoirs written by members of your class.

 Decide what are the key features that make these recounts effective. Be prepared to feed your ideas back to the class.

Now write up to three targets for the next time you write a recount text.

C The Art of Information Writing

How information text works

AIMS

- Revisit the key ingredients of information text.
- Use a text skeleton to analyse the structure of information text.

In this section you will build on your existing knowledge of how an information text works, thinking about its audience, purpose and form, and focusing on its typical structure and language features.

Audience, purpose, form

Information texts tell us about the key characteristics of places, people, animals, ideas or things. Some typical examples of information texts are:

- **dictionaries**, which give you information about the spelling and usage of words
- **reference books**, such as one on the rocks and minerals of the British Isles
- **information sheets**, such as one on HIV/AIDS in a health clinic.

TYPICAL FEATURES

The typical features of information texts are listed below. You will need to refer to these in Section 2.

The **audience** is someone who wants to know about something.

The **purpose** is to present information so that it is easy to find and understand.

The **form** or structure of information text often includes an introduction which gives general statements about the topic; paragraphs or sections in logical order (often organised in topics related to the main subject with subheadings); topic sentences to introduce key points (usually the first sentence of a paragraph); and tables, diagrams, glossary, notes and icons[1] to add information or replace text.

Typical **language features** are:

- formal and impersonal language, e.g. 'Visual signals are used for communication'
- technical terms relating to subject matter, and precise vocabulary, e.g. 'different species'
- present tense to describe how things are, e.g. 'Animals communicate'
- opening sentences that are often general statements, e.g. 'Sound is the most common form'
- specific detail to illustrate the general points, e.g. 'Birdsong, for example'
- clear, concise sentences – though descriptive language can be appropriate.

[1] **icon** – a small picture or symbol

The first dictionary entry below has been annotated to illustrate the language features and structure of an information text. Read the extract and annotations carefully, then annotate the other two entries to show where the same elements occur.

Present tense

Clear and concise sentence

Clear headword
– this topic heading shows word entry

Icon – shows topics related to main subject

Formal and impersonal language

Precise vocabulary

General statement – followed by additional detailed information

Technical term

Paragraphs (entries) in alphabetical order

graffiti
Said "graf-**fee**-tee" NOUN Graffiti is slogans or drawings scribbled on walls.
from Italian *graffiare* meaning 'to scratch a surface'
Although *graffiti* is a plural in Italian, the language it comes from, in English it can be used as a singular noun or a plural noun.

greet greets greeting greeted
VERB **1** If you greet someone, you say something friendly like 'hello' to them when you meet them.
2 If you greet something in a particular way, you react to it in that way E.G. *He was greeted with deep suspicion.*
(sense 1) hail, salute

grimace grimaces grimacing grimaced
Said "grim-**mace**" NOUN **1** a twisted facial expression indicating disgust or pain. ▶ VERB **2** When someone grimaces, they make a grimace.

In dictionaries, headwords (topic headings) are used instead of topic sentences. The headwords have been highlighted in orange in the extract above. Discuss:

- Why headwords are so important in a dictionary.
- Why it is this important that each entry presents information in the same order.

Be prepared to share your conclusions.

Using text skeletons

In order to understand the structure of a text, it can be useful to draw a diagram or 'text skeleton'. Text skeletons represent the bare bones of a text.

A typical information skeleton is a spidergram. In the skeleton for 'graffiti' below, each bubble surrounding the subject in the centre represents a particular topic relating to the main subject. (In longer information texts these bubbles often sum up a single paragraph or section.) The lines branching from each bubble are memory joggers, which are further points connected to the main topic, for example, 'from Italian'.

Using text skeletons will help you both to analyse the structure of a text and to plan your own writing.

Task 3 ⟩ **Structuring** ━━━━━━━━━━━━━━━

Below is a completed text skeleton for the dictionary entry for 'graffiti'. Work out how you would compose a text skeleton to sum up the entry for 'grimace'.

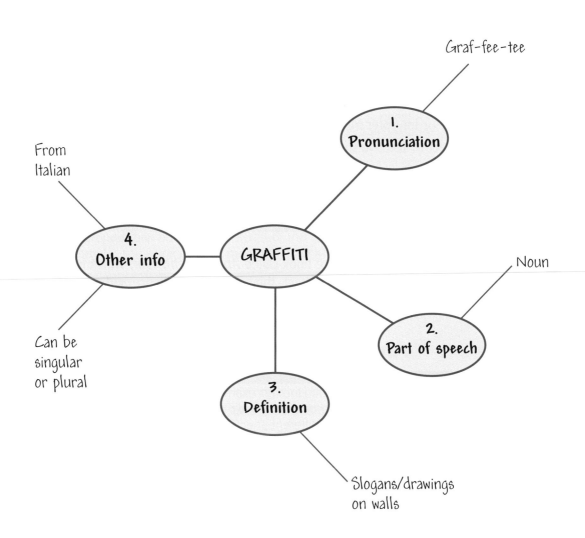

Features of information text

The first half of the extract on pages 38–39 has been annotated to show some of the key features of information texts. Note that descriptive language is a feature of this kind of information text, unlike the dictionary extracts that you analysed in Section 1. Refer back to the Typical Features panel on page 35.

 Task 6 **Annotating**

 Annotate the second half of the text to illustrate as many other examples of these features as possible.

Adding glosses

Information texts often use specialist or technical vocabulary. Rather than explain each term as it comes up, the writer explains any common terms in a separate glossary box. Glossaries either list terms in alphabetical order or in the order in which they appear in the text.

Task 7 **Discussing**

 Glossary entries should be both clear and concise (short). Discuss what is wrong with the following gloss. Refer back to the original gloss on page 39.

> **arthropod** – insects are arthropods, and they aren't the only ones. An arthropod is an animal. It has jointed limbs and an outside skeleton. Spiders are as well.

Task 8 **Writing**

Draft a clear and concise gloss to explain either 'tabloid newspaper' or 'broadsheet newspaper'. Your audience is 8- to 11-year-olds. Here is some information that may be useful.

TABLOID FACTS

- *The Sun, Daily Mirror* and *Daily Mail* are all tabloid newspapers.
- Tabloid newspapers have more photos and less text than broadsheet newspapers.
- They often have a more sensational style, with the emphasis on entertainment.
- The front-page headlines are bigger.
- The pages measure about 40 x 30cm.

BROADSHEET FACTS

- The *Times, The Guardian* and *The Independent* are all broadsheet newspapers.
- Broadsheet newspapers have fewer photos and more text than tabloids.
- They have a more reasoned style, with an emphasis on news and comment.
- The front-page headlines are smaller than those in the tabloids.
- The pages often measure about 61 x 38cm, but some also produce a 'tabloid-sized' version.

Formal language

Most information writing uses formal language. This is for two reasons:

- to show that it is serious
- to make it as clear as possible.

The two sentences below remind you of the features of formal and informal language.

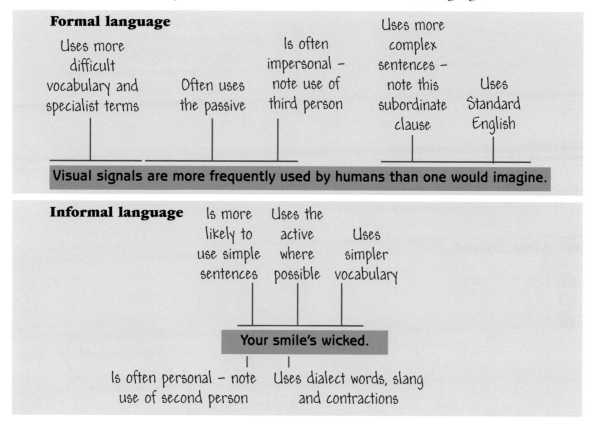

Formal language

Uses more difficult vocabulary and specialist terms

Often uses the passive

Is often impersonal – note use of third person

Uses more complex sentences – note this subordinate clause

Uses Standard English

Visual signals are more frequently used by humans than one would imagine.

Informal language

Is more likely to use simple sentences

Uses the active where possible

Uses simpler vocabulary

Your smile's wicked.

Is often personal – note use of second person

Uses dialect words, slang and contractions

Task 9 — Formal language

Identify at least five examples of formal language in the *Animal Communication* extract.

Task 10 — Writing

The Museum of Communications has produced some information for new visitors to the museum, but it is too informal, and the Director has asked you to make it more formal.

Start by looking back at the features of formal language above. As you rewrite the information, you may want to alter the order, as well as the words and structure, of the sentences.

Here are some sentence signposts that you could use:

- The Museum of Communications is a fascinating collection of …
- Visitors will be able to see …
- The famous inventor Thomas Edison …

Welcome to Alexander Graham Bell's first telephone, and so much more!

How can you resist this collection of over 100 antique radios, printing presses, cameras and TVs? You'll enjoy a trip down memory lane – and beyond! – as you see how the printing press works, and the telephone of course. You'll also meet those great inventors who made our world such a small place! Famous Tom Edison is our computer-generated cyberguide through this fantabulous museum.

Your kids, grandkids, and pals will all enjoy the show!

And bring your cameras – you're allowed to snap away for free!

The Art of Information Writing

Getting the structure right

AIMS

- Analyse the overall structure of a text, using a text skeleton, to identify how key ideas are developed.

- Group sentences into paragraphs by adding or exemplifying a point.

In this section you will use a text skeleton to help analyse the structure of the reference text on animal communication, and to structure it in a different way. You will also think about how to keep your paragraphs focused and well developed.

Creating a text skeleton

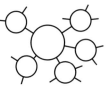

Text skeletons sum up the structure of a text in a visual way (see page 37). The skeleton for information texts will help you understand the structure of the reference text on animal communication.

Task 11 | **Structuring**

 Look at the text skeleton for the beginning of *the Animal Communication* extract below. Complete the skeleton for the rest of the extract. Use the subheadings to help you.

5.

4.

ANIMAL COMMUNICATION

1. Introduction

— Animals communicate with own species – food, danger, territory

— With other species – warning off

— Three ways of communicating: sounds, sight, smell

2. Sound

— Common form

— Lots of information

3.

Focusing and developing paragraphs

Paragraphs in information texts often begin with topic sentences that are rather bare, general statements. These statements are then fleshed out by adding detail or examples as the paragraph is developed. The writer signals additions to a point, or further examples, by using conjunctions, sentence connectives or sentence signposts. This makes the text cohesive, or holds together well. (For an explanation of these terms, see page 87.)

Signalling additions and examples

Adding to a point		Giving examples	
and	also	such as	This can be seen in
also	Moreover	including	This is illustrated by
in addition	What is more	for instance	Examples include
Furthermore	A further feature is	similarly	just as
besides	as well	for example	In the same way

The Art of Information Writing

Task 12 **Analysing**

Look at the extract below and discuss these questions.

- Which general statement is the main focus of the paragraph?
- Where are details added and where are examples given?
- Which signposts has the writer used to show exactly where the paragraph is going?
- How does the conjunction 'although' in the first sentence differ from the others?

> Visual signals are also used for communication, although they only work at relatively close range. For instance, when a cat arches its back and makes its hair stand on end, she is attempting to frighten you off. Similarly, the black and white stripes of a skunk warn a mountain lion not to come too close or it will be squirted with its evil-smelling spray. Chimpanzees and apes can even communicate their feelings through facial expressions – just as humans do.

Task 13 **Planning practice**

You are planning an encyclopedia entry for the term 'media'. Media are the different ways in which people communicate information to others, such as newspapers and television. The notice board below shows some of the main topics that you need to cover (in bold), together with additional information and examples. First, decide how you will order these points for the media entry. Then draw up a text skeleton, putting your main points in numbered bubbles and using memory joggers to give examples or additional information.

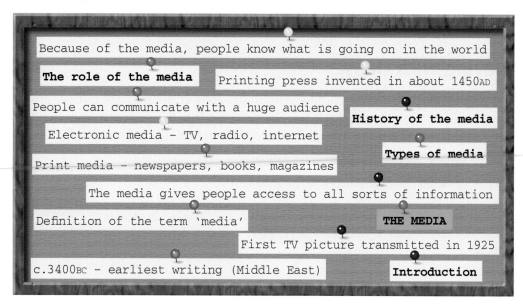

Because of the media, people know what is going on in the world

The role of the media   Printing press invented in about 1450AD

People can communicate with a huge audience

Electronic media – TV, radio, internet   **History of the media**

Print media – newspapers, books, magazines   **Types of media**

The media gives people access to all sorts of information

Definition of the term 'media'   THE MEDIA

First TV picture transmitted in 1925

c.3400BC – earliest writing (Middle East)   **Introduction**

Task 14 **Writing**

Draft one paragraph of the entry, which focuses on the different kinds of media. Begin with a clear statement of what the focus of the paragraph is about, develop it with examples and further detail, and use signposts to show where the paragraph is going, as in the table on page 42.

You may want to add information and examples that are not on the notice board above.

The Art of Information Writing

Making the sentences work

AIMS

- Investigate non-finite clauses as a means of adding variety to sentence structures, and how to punctuate them correctly.

- Extend the range of prepositions and connectives used to indicate purpose.

- Explore the use of the dash as a punctuation mark.

In this section you will explore how to use non-finite clauses and think about how punctuation can help you express your meaning.

Non-finite clauses

The underlined clause in this sentence from *Animal Communication* is a non-finite clause.

> The young bird learns the song from its neighbours, <u>breaking it down into segments</u> so that it is easier for him to memorise it.

Non-finite clauses are another way of structuring sentences to add variety to your writing and detail to information texts. They can go at the front, the back or in the middle of sentences.

- <u>Busily singing its song</u>, the young bird didn't notice the cat.
- The young bird, <u>busily singing its song</u>, didn't notice the cat.

Task 15 | **Playing with clauses**

 The order and content of a sentence with a non-finite or subordinate clause can be changed to alter the emphasis and/or meaning (see the grammar panel on page 45). Look carefully at the ways in which the following sentence has been changed.

Snapping at his heels, the dog chased him home.

> Place the main clause first, e.g. 'The dog chased him home, snapping at his heels.'
> Move the verb in the subordinate clause, e.g. 'The dog chased him home, <u>nipping</u> at his heels.'
> Change the subject in the main clause, e.g. 'The <u>goat</u> chased him home, snapping at his heels.'
> Change the verb in the main clause, e.g. 'The dog <u>followed</u> him home, snapping at his heels.'
> Place the subordinate clause in the middle of the sentence, e.g. 'The dog, <u>snapping at his heels</u>, chased him home.'

Now try playing with the following sentence as shown above. Note: The new sentence must make sense.

Hissing loudly, the angry cat was backed into a corner.

Non-finite clauses are clauses with incomplete **verb phrases**, such as 'to smile', 'having run', 'exhausted', 'singing'. Non-finite clauses are subordinate clauses, which do not make sense on their own.

The non-finite clauses are underlined in the examples below, and the verb phrase is in bold. The main clause is the non-underlined part of the sentence. Note: A comma is almost always used to separate the clauses.

- He walked away, **smiling** bitterly.

- **To get** top marks, you'll have to work really hard.

- **Disappointed** with himself, he turned for home.

Indicating purpose

Task 16 | Analysing and discussing

 Look carefully at the pairs of sentences below. Discuss:

- Which one of each pair tells you more about the relationship between the first and second clauses?

- Can you explain that relationship?

- How do the sentences make this clear?

Pair A
- The hawk moth reveals two huge eyespots **and** suggests a much bigger and fiercer creature.

- The hawk moth reveals two huge eyespots **to** suggest a much bigger and fiercer creature.

Pair B
- The bird breaks the song into segments **and** it is easier for him to memorise it.

- The bird breaks the song into segments **so that** it is easier for him to memorise it.

Top tip The conjunction 'and' does not usually bring out the best links between clauses.

There are many ways of indicating purpose in a complex sentence. The following conjunctions can all introduce a subordinate clause, which expresses the idea of purpose:

• so that	• with the intention of
• to	• with the purpose of
• in order to	• for the purpose of
• in order that	• with a view to

The Art of Information Writing

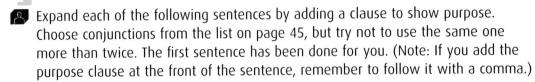

Expand each of the following sentences by adding a clause to show purpose. Choose conjunctions from the list on page 45, but try not to use the same one more than twice. The first sentence has been done for you. (Note: If you add the purpose clause at the front of the sentence, remember to follow it with a comma.)

1. John looked on the Internet.
   John looked on the Internet find information about India.

3. Engineers assess the performance of each television.

4. They launched the film just before Christmas.

5. The company sold off its newspaper business.

Using the dash

The punctuation mark – (the dash) can be a very useful tool for giving structure to a sentence.

Task 18 **Recording**

Several dashes have been used in the *Animal Communication* extract on pages 38–39. Identify where dashes have been used, and why. Then discuss how effective they are at making the meaning of the sentence clear.

GRAMMAR

The **dash** can be used for two main purposes, to *interrupt* a sentence and to *extend* a sentence.

1. Dashes can interrupt sentences by marking off extra information in the sentence, for example:
   It is a useful – perhaps even the best – way of recording information.

Note: This is often a better alternative to enclosing the information in commas or in brackets. Using dashes in this way can have the effect of drawing more attention to the words that are set off from the rest of the sentence.

2. Dashes can also extend sentences by adding an extra word, phrase or clause, for example:
   It's a bird – a really big bird.
   It's a bird – and I thought it was a plane.

Note: Here, too, the dash has the effect of emphasising the extra material.

Top tip

- Use dashes sparingly – too many dashes make your sentences very jerky – like this – and hard to follow.
- Make sure that if you are using dashes to mark off information, you use them in pairs. The following sentence is not punctuated correctly:

  It is a useful way – perhaps even the best, of recording information.

Your task

Write a clear information text about how humans communicate.

AIMS

- Plan, draft and present an information text, selecting appropriate material and guiding the reader through the text.

- Adapt the conventions and formality of information text to fit a particular audience and purpose.

- Reread and revise the work to anticipate the effect on the reader.

Test watch This writing task is good preparation for the type of writing required in your English tests because it helps you learn how to:

- plan your work so that it is organised logically into well-constructed paragraphs that are coherently linked together

- compose your writing effectively to match its audience and purpose,

- selecting powerful vocabulary

- vary the structure of your sentences and punctuate them correctly.

If you show these skills in the optional English test at the end of Year 8, you will gain a better mark.

1 Audience and purpose

 A space probe containing all sorts of information about life on Earth is to be sent to Mars. Your task is to write the section that describes how humans communicate. Your audience is the Martian who discovers the probe. Your purpose is to give this alien clear information about different forms of communication.

Discuss what effect the audience and purpose of this task will have on the style. In particular, consider these questions:

- How will you help the Martian understand the specialist terms?

- How formal and impersonal should the language be?

- Would you include a humorous element, poking fun at humans?

2 Brainstorming the content

 Brainstorm all the ways in which people communicate, e.g. body language. Give examples of each form of communication

and its purpose, e.g. shouting shows concern, anger or that the other person is distant.

3 Planning the form and structure

  Use the brainstorm to decide what you want to cover in your piece of writing.

List the main topics in the most effective order. Then use these topics to

create an information skeleton. Begin your information text with an introduction explaining the topics to be covered.

The Art of Information Writing

Composing your piece

Now you are ready to start writing.

Points to remember

As you write, remember to:

- keep your audience and purpose in mind (see page 35)
- keep your sentences clear and straightforward, but include some lively description
- select a style with the appropriate formality (see page 41)
- include clear and concise explanations of technical or specialist terms in a short glossary (see page 40)
- give each paragraph a focus, using topic sentences (see page 42)
- develop the paragraph with examples and related points, signposting this so the reader doesn't get lost (see page 42)
- use complex sentences, especially non-finite and purpose clauses, to make your writing varied and the connection between ideas clear (see page 44)
- make sure that your punctuation helps the reader follow the sense of your sentences, especially when you use commas and dashes (see page 46).

You may want to use some of the sentence signposts and connectives below to help you.

Sentence signposts and connectives
- There are several ways
- One common form of communication
- Other signals include clothes, gestures and
- Human clothing also communicates
- Furthermore
- As well
- Another feature that
- In addition
- For example
- In the same way
- Including

Peer comment

 Swap your draft with a partner's and read it carefully. Decide what works well and highlight this on the draft. Discuss how to improve your partner's information text. Write up to three suggestions on the draft.

Redraft the selected sections of your text, using your partner's comments to guide you.

Pulling it all together

 Listen to the pieces written by members of your class.

 Decide what are the key features that make these extracts effective.

Be prepared to feed back your ideas to the class.

Set up to three targets for yourself for improving your next piece of information writing.

D The Art of Explanation Writing

1 How explanation text works

AIMS

- Revisit the key ingredients of explanation text.
- Use a text skeleton to analyse the structure of explanation text.

In this section you will build on your existing knowledge of how an explanation text works, thinking about its audience, purpose and form, and focusing on its typical structure and language features.

Audience, purpose and form

Explanation texts help you understand how or why something happens – showing how one thing can cause another or how something works. Some typical examples are:

- **geography essays**, which could, for example, answer the question 'What causes volcanoes to erupt?'
- **science textbooks**, which could explain how muscles help the body to move
- **letters**, e.g. from a parent excusing their child from a games lesson.

Although explanation texts often include a lot of information, they differ from information texts. Information texts focus on telling you *what* things are like, whereas explanation texts focus on explaining *how* or *why* they are as they are.

The typical features of explanation texts are listed below. You will need to refer to these in Section 2.

TYPICAL FEATURES

- The **audience** is someone who wants to understand a process.
- Its **purpose** is to help someone understand a process.
- The **form** or structure that an explanation text often takes is a series of logical steps explaining how or why something occurs (cause and effect). It may include bullet points, subheadings or numbers (to make the steps clear); topic sentences to introduce each step; diagrams or illustrations.

Typical **language features** of explanation texts are:

- causal[1] language including sentence signposts, conjunctions and connectives, e.g. 'This is caused by', 'because', 'as a result', 'therefore'
- technical and precise vocabulary (a glossary may be needed)
- formal and impersonal language (often including the passive), e.g. 'Writing was invented around the middle of the fourth millennium'
- present tense for generalising[2] (past tense if explaining events in the past), e.g. 'Sound waves are'
- similes or metaphors for comparing an idea with something more familiar to the reader, e.g. 'Your ears, which act a bit like satellite dishes'

[1] **causal** – stating or implying a cause (why or how something happens)

[2] **generalising** – making a general statement (e.g. about all cats) rather than a statement about one example (e.g. your cat)

The first half of the extract below has been annotated to illustrate some of the language features of an explanation text. Read the text and annotations carefully, then annotate the second half to show more examples of these ingredients and comment on their effects.

Title – introduces what is being explained

Use of the passive

Causal language

Structure – a series of logical steps. The second paragraph begins to answer the question posed in the first

Topic sentence – introduces a step in the explanation

Past tense – because explaining events in the past

Technical vocabulary – referring to particular time period

Formal and impersonal language

Why was Writing Invented?

So far we have investigated when writing was invented, and what forms early writing took; but why did we begin to write at all? What was it that drove our ancestors to take this momentous step, which would change forever the nature of communication?

By the middle of the fourth millennium BC, society in the Near East (modern Iraq) had become increasingly complex, with its laws and trading patterns and technical achievements. It was, therefore, more and more important to communicate facts and, above all, to have a record of these facts.

Making a mark on a piece of clay had two great advantages over holding the same information in the brain. First, the writer no longer had to remember what he had written down. And second, the clay became a permanent message, which stayed around whether the messenger was there or not (or even after he had died). Instead of saying, therefore, 'I own two oxen,' the writer could make a mark in a piece of clay which recorded the fact for all to see.

Topic sentences

Topic sentences are used to introduce the key focus of each paragraph. They are often the first sentence of a paragraph. If you summarise the topic sentences, you get a picture of the whole passage.

Task 2 **Summarising**

Complete the summary below by adding the key focus of the last paragraph. You will need to identify the topic sentence.

Paragraph 1: Why did we begin to write?

Paragraph 2: Society in Near East more complex by 3500BC

Paragraph 3:

Using text skeletons

In order to understand the structure of a text, it can be useful to draw a diagram or 'text skeleton'. Text skeletons represent the bare bones of the text.

A typical explanation skeleton, showing how one thing leads to another, is given below. Each bubble represents one stage in the explanation. In this case the first paragraph provides an introduction and the next two paragraphs provide the first two stages in the explanation.

The three bubbles on the skeleton represent these three sections of the text. The notes in each bubble give the focus of the paragraph, for example 'A momentous step'. The lines branching from each bubble are its key related points, for example 'have already explored 'when' and 'what'. These notes are known as memory joggers.

Using text skeletons will help you to analyse the structure and content of a text, and plan your own writing.

Task 3 **Structuring**

Below is a partially-completed text skeleton for *Why was Writing Invented?* Work out how you would complete the third bubble and its memory joggers to sum up the final paragraph.

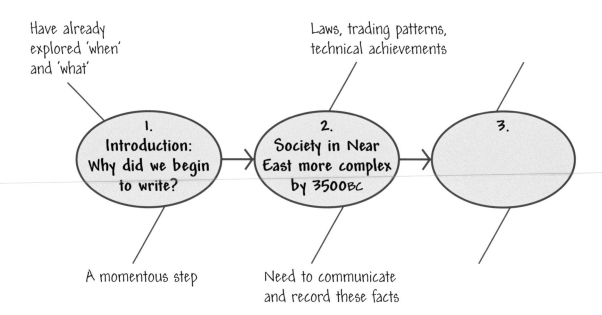

Have already explored 'when' and 'what'

Laws, trading patterns, technical achievements

1.
Introduction: Why did we begin to write?

2.
Society in Near East more complex by 3500BC

3.

A momentous step

Need to communicate and record these facts

Learning from example

AIMS

- Review the vocabulary, sentence grammar and stylistic conventions of explanation text.

- Make notes in different ways, choosing a form which suits the purpose.

- Think about how writers can use figurative language and comparisons to make complex ideas understandable.

In this section you will focus on an explanation text and think about what techniques the writer has used to help the reader understand the process described, as well as engaging the reader's interest.

Test watch As well as building up your writing skills, the following sections are good preparation for the optional reading tests at the end of Year 8 because they help you:

- comment on a writer's purpose and the effects of the text on the reader

- comment on the structure and organisation of texts

- comment on writers' use of language

- deduce, infer or interpret information, events or ideas

- describe, select or retrieve information, events or ideas from texts.

If you show these skills in the reading test, you will gain a better mark.

Task 4 ## Reading

 The extract on page 53 is from a young people's science book, which explains how your body works. While reading the extract, discuss the following questions:

- Which language features make this an explanation text?

- Which features of the form and stucture help you understand the process being explained?

Task 5 ## Topic sentences

 Consider what the text is about. Start by looking at the topic sentences, the first two of which have been highlighted in orange. Identify the remaining topic sentences. Be prepared to use these sentences to summarise the extract for the rest of the class.

Task 6 **Annotating**

 The first two paragraphs of the extract have been annotated to illustrate all the ingredients of explanation texts, see the Typical Features panel on page 49.

Read the text and annotations carefully. Annotate the final four paragraphs to bring out all these features.

Diagram – makes the explanation clear

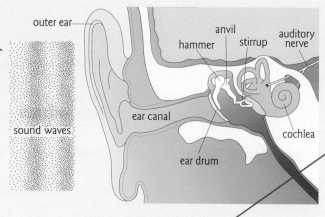

outer ear

anvil
hammer stirrup auditory nerve

ear canal

cochlea

ear drum

sound waves

Title – introduces what is being explained

Causal language

How We Hear Sounds

Present tense – explaining how things are

Formal and impersonal language – includes the passive

Precise technical vocabulary

Sound waves <u>are</u> ripples of vibration in the air. <u>When a guitar string is plucked</u>, for example, <u>it vibrates rapidly, and these vibrations are sent through the air as ripples, or sound waves</u>. Your ears, <u>which act a bit like satellite dishes</u>, gather up the sound waves and channel them into your ear canal. All this occurs in what is called the <u>outer ear</u>.

<u>At the end of the ear canal the sound waves reach the eardrum</u>, which is the entrance to the <u>middle ear</u>. The eardrum is just like a real drum: a thin wall of skin which vibrates as the sound waves hit it. <u>If the sounds are high, the eardrum vibrates rapidly; if they are low</u>, it vibrates slowly; in this way the eardrum <u>faithfully preserves the complex mix of vibrations that make up any sound</u>.

Simile – compares process with something similar

5

Topic sentence – introduces next step in the explanation

10 **Causal language**

Structure – a series of logical steps. Each paragraph adds the next piece of the explanation

The vibrations of the eardrum set up further vibrations in a chain of three tiny bones – the hammer, anvil and stirrup. These are arranged in such a way that by the time the vibrations reach the end of the third bone, the stirrup, they have been amplified[1] hugely. They are able to do this rather like a system of levers is able to turn a small movement at one end into a huge and powerful movement at the other.

Formal and impersonal language

15

The sound wave, in the form of the tiny stirrup's powerful vibrations, has now reached the entrance to the inner ear. The inner ear is basically a set of three tubes, together called the cochlea, which wind round each other in a spiral so that they look a bit like a snail's shell. The cochlea is full of fluid, and as the stirrup knocks on what is called the oval window of the cochlea, the fluid within – yes, you've guessed it – vibrates.

20

[1] **amplified** – made louder

The actual organ of hearing, known as the Organ of Corti, lies hidden in the central tube of the cochlea. It contains over 15 000 hair cells. The pressure waves moving through the fluid of the cochlea wash over these highly sensitive cells, and as the hairs waggle and wave like strands of seaweed in the sea, they send electrical signals to the brain along the cochleal nerve. 25

The signals preserve the correct frequency[2] of the original sound, because different hair cells are affected by different frequencies. They also preserve the correct volume of the sound, because more hair cells are affected when the volume of the sound is higher. So when the brain receives these signals at the end of their lightning-fast and breathless underground journey, it interprets them as sounds of a precise frequency and volume. It can tell, for example, that the guitar string that was plucked was an A, and that it was plucked very softly. 30 35

[2] **frequency** – the rate at which a sound vibrates, which determines how high or low the sound is

Writing clearly

The writer of an explanation text often has to explain complex ideas. The key to explaining complex ideas is to write clearly.

One way of doing this is to keep your sentences plain and simple:

- Keep your sentences to a short or medium length.
- Introduce the subject of the sentence early.
- Use straightforward verbs so that the reader knows what is happening.

GRAMMAR

subject – the person or thing performing the action of the sentence. For example, in the sentence *The inner ear is a set of three tubes*, the subject is 'The inner ear'. See also page 104.

Task 7 **Analysing**

 Scan *How We Hear Sounds* for examples of clear writing. Discuss why each example is effective. Be prepared to share your findings with the class.

Writing imaginatively

If explanation texts were completely plain and simple, however, they would not be doing their job well. The explanation would be too dull to interest the reader.

For this reason, using a lively image can both brighten up an explanation and help to relate it to the reader's experience. Figurative language,[1] such as metaphors[2] and especially similes,[3] is also very useful in this respect.

Descriptive writing doesn't only occur in narrative and recount texts. In fact, selecting just the right words to describe something powerfully is an important ingredient of most forms of writing.

[1] **figurative language** – language that uses images, or pictures, to compare one thing with another

[2] **metaphor** – when one thing is said to be another, e.g. 'sound waves are ripples of sound'

[3] **simile** – when one thing is compared to another with the words 'like' or 'as', e.g. 'the eardrum is like a real drum'

Task 8 — Figurative language

 How has the writer of *How We Hear Sounds* used figurative language to make the explanation both clearer and more interesting? Draw up and complete a table like the one below. Try to find at least six examples – though there are at least ten in the extract.

Figurative language used	Metaphor/simile	Effect
'Sound waves are ripples of vibration'	Metaphor	It makes you 'see' the sound, a bit like ripples in water
'ears act a bit like satellite dishes'	Simile	

Task 9 — Discussing

 Below is a children's encyclopedia explanation for why thunder usually rumbles (the sound lasts a long time) rather than making a single sudden sound.

> Air is rapidly heated by the lightning flash. As the air violently expands, it causes the sound of thunder. Thunder rumbles because of the time difference between the sounds originating from the nearer and the further parts of the lightning flash.

Discuss how you would explain the rumbling of thunder in a lively and relevant way. You may like to compare it to an avalanche, or to your stomach rumbling.

Remember to keep your audience in mind.

Getting the structure right

AIMS

- Make notes in different ways, choosing a form which suits the purpose.

- Analyse the overall structure of a text to identify how key ideas are developed.

- Explain complex ideas clearly, linking sentences to signal the stage in the process.

In this section you will use a text skeleton to analyse the structure of an explanation text, and think about what helps the reader understand the exact stages in the process.

Understanding text skeletons

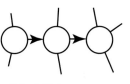

Text skeletons sum up the structure of a text in a visual way (see page 51). The skeleton for an explanation text helps you understand the structure of the passage *How We Hear Sounds*.

Task 10 | **Structuring**

Look at the text skeleton for the beginning of the passage below. Complete the skeleton for the rest of the passage. The skeleton will have six bubbles to match the six paragraphs in *How We Hear Sounds* (see page 53–54). Use the topic sentences you identified to help (see page 52).

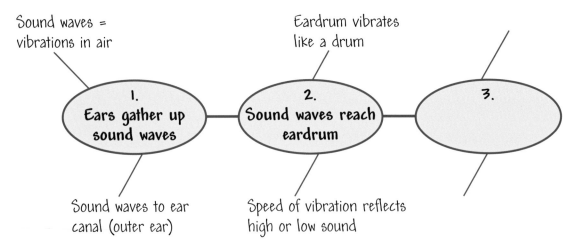

Signposting the process

When an explanation is complex and involves some unfamiliar words or ideas, it is important to help the reader find their way around the text. There are various ways of doing this, but two of them are highlighted in the extract at the top of page 57:

- **Repeating or referring to key words** to signal where the explanation is going.
- **Setting the scene** – indicating clearly what stage the process has reached.

> Sound waves are ripples of vibration in the air. When a guitar string is plucked, for example, it vibrates rapidly, and <u>these vibrations</u> are sent through the air as ripples, or sound waves. Your ears, which act a bit like satellite dishes, gather up the sound waves and channel them into your ear canal. <u>All this</u> occurs in what is called the outer ear.
>
> <u>At the end of the ear canal</u> the sound waves reach the eardrum, which marks the entrance to the middle ear. <u>The eardrum</u> is just like...

Refers back to 'it vibrates'

Refers back to previous sentence and sums up

Sets the scene at the beginning of new paragraph

Repeats key noun and uses it to start new sentence

Task 11 Annotating

Look through the rest of the passage carefully and identify further examples where the writer has set the scene or signposted a key word in this way. Jot down your examples in a table, or annotate a copy of the passage.

The opening phrases in each paragraph act as signposts in this way. Why do you think this is?

Task 12 Planning practice

Imagine that you are writing a book for young children explaining how things work. Your task is to plan the section: 'How a letter gets from your Gran's writing desk to your breakfast table'. This will explain clearly in three or four short paragraphs exactly what happens in the process of sending a letter.

Begin by rearranging the key events (see right) so that they are in the correct order to describe the process. Then turn this into an explanation skeleton, adding memory joggers for supporting information.

A Postman puts letter through your door
B Letters sorted again – by road
C Puts letter in envelope
D Addresses envelope to you
E Letters sorted by town
F Puts stamp on envelope
G Takes letters in van to sorting office
H Dad puts letter on breakfast table
I Postman collects letters from postbox
J Gran writes letter
K Letters taken by road/rail to their destination
L Posts letter in postbox

Now draft the explanation, which covers everything up to the posting of the letter. As you draft your paragraphs, focus on making the links between the ideas clear by:

- adding causal connectives where appropriate to explain why each step is necessary, e.g. 'She puts a stamp on the envelope because'
- giving each paragraph a clear topic sentence, e.g. 'The letters are sorted into their different destinations at a place called a sorting office'
- signposting the process by repeating key words or setting the scene, e.g. 'This envelope'.

Share your draft with a partner and discuss how it might be improved.

The Art of Explanation Writing

Making the sentences work

AIMS

- Explore different ways of highlighting cause and effect in sentences.

- Practise using relative clauses, paying attention to the use of the comma as a boundary signpost.

- Use semicolons and other kinds of punctuation to avoid the comma splice.

In this section you will explore ways of highlighting cause-and-effect links in explanation texts. You will also review relative clauses and focus on the use (and misuse) of the comma.

Highlighting cause and effect

Cause-and-effect links are particularly important in explanation texts. The passage *How We Hear Sounds* highlights some of the links between cause and effect:

GRAMMAR

1. By using **conjunctions** to link clauses.
- *When a guitar string is plucked, it vibrates rapidly.*
- *If the sounds are high, the eardrum vibrates rapidly*
- *...wind round each other in a spiral so that...*
- *...as the hairs waggle...,they send...*

2. By using **sentence connectives** to link parts of sentences or whole sentences.
- *So when the brain receives these signals...*
- *When the brain receives these signals, therefore,...*

3. By using **sentence signposts** to show where a sentence is going.
- *The vibrations of the eardrum set up further vibrations...*
- *These are arranged in such a way that...*

(For more on these features, see the explanation of cohesion on page 87.)

(For more on these features, see the explanation of cohesion on page 87.)

Task 13 | **Writing**

 Look at the following two statements:

- *Rob's letter got lost in the post.*
- *He sent an email instead.*

Here are three ways of combining the statements to bring out the cause and effect:

For example:

Using conjunction

- *1 Rob sent an email <u>because</u> his letter got lost in the post.*

Using sentence connective

- *2. Rob's letter got lost in the post. <u>Therefore</u> he sent an email instead.*

Using sentence signpost

- *3. <u>The reason why</u> Rob sent an email is that his letter got lost in the post.*

Find two more ways to combine the statements. Underline the cause-and-effect links in your sentences, as in the examples above. You may have to alter the wording of the two original sentences.

Using the relative clause

Relative clauses are very useful when you want to extend a sentence by adding extra information to a noun or noun phrase. They can also help to add detail in explanation text. For example:

- *Your ears, **which act a bit like satellite dishes**, gather up…*
- *…the eardrum, **which marks the entrance to the middle ear**.*
- *The eardrum is just like a real drum: a thin wall of skin **which vibrates as the sound waves hit it**.*

GRAMMAR

A relative clause gives extra information about the noun or noun phrase to which it is attached. Relative clauses are introduced by the **relative pronouns** 'who', 'which', 'whom', 'whose' or 'that'.

1. A relative clause often provides additional information (as in the first two examples in the bullet list above), in which case it is separated from the main clause by a comma.

2. Some relative clauses, however, provide information that is necessary for a full understanding of the sentence (as in the third bulleted example above), in which case there is no comma separating the clause.

Task 14 **Writing**

 Link each of the following pairs of sentences by using a relative clause, as shown in the first example. You may need to miss out a word or two when you combine the sentences, and you may need to change the order of the clauses.

Then check the punctuation. Do you need to mark off the clause with commas?

1. The first letter never arrived. I wrote it to you.
   The first letter that I wrote to you never arrived.

2. I thought of using email. Email is much faster.

3. Texting is best of all. It is an even newer way of communicating.

4. My grandmother uses email. She is nearly 91.

5. I have lost the telephone number. You gave me that number yesterday.

Avoiding the comma splice

Look at these two main clauses:

- *At the end of the ear canal the sound waves reach the eardrum.*
- *This marks the entrance to the middle ear.*

There are several ways of linking these main clauses in a single sentence. For example, by using:

- **a colon:** *...the sound waves reach the eardrum: this marks the...*
- **a semicolon:** *...the sound waves reach the eardrum; this marks the....*
- **a dash:** *...the sound waves reach the eardrum – this marks the...*
- **a conjunction:** *...the sound waves reach the eardrum, and this marks the...*
- **a relative clause:** *...the sound waves reach the eardrum, which marks the...*

What you should NOT do is to join the two main clauses with a comma:

- *...the sound waves reach the eardrum, this marks the...*

This is called the **comma splice**. This shouldn't be used because it does not show the connection between the two clauses. Instead it creates a weak sentence without any direction.

Task 15 Discussing

In the passage below the writer has used the comma splice at least once in every sentence. What is the effect?

Discuss with a partner how you could punctuate this passage to make the connections between clauses clear. You will also need to change some of the wording. Look at the grammar panels on pages 59 and 60 for help.

> Mailing lists can also be used as a form of online chat between friends, they are, however, not as immediate as chat programs, they don't work in 'real time'. Mailing lists are usually handled by a 'list server', it is a special program that automatically sorts the incoming messages, it then sends them out to all the current list subscribers. That can be a lot of messages, it is important not to subscribe to too many lists, you may end up with hundreds of messages every day.

5 Composing an explanation

AIMS

- Plan, draft and finalise a text explaining complex ideas and information clearly.

- Adapt the conventions and formality of explanation text to fit a particular audience and purpose.

- Reread and revise the work to anticipate the effect on the reader.

Your task

Write a clear explanation of why a dictionary is structured the way it is.

Test watch This writing task is good preparation for the type of writing required in your English tests because it helps you learn how to:

- plan your work so that it is organised logically into well constructed paragraphs that are coherently linked together

- compose your writing effectively to match its audience and purpose

- selecting appropriate vocabulary

- structure your sentences appropriately and punctuate them correctly.

If you show these skills in the optional English test at the end of Year 8, you will gain a better mark.

Audience, purpose and form

Your task is to write a clear explanation of the structure of your class dictionary. This means that you have to explain both *how* the dictionary is structured and *why* it has this structure. Your audience is other people of your age.

Thinking about the content

 Look carefully at your class dictionary and research with a partner the questions in the boxes below. Make short notes from your research for later.

Focusing on the whole book

- What different sections make up your dictionary? (For example, list of words, how to use, preface, introduction, appendixes.)

- Why are they included?

- What order are they in and why?

Focusing on the entries section

- How are the dictionary entries ordered? If they are ordered alphabetically, why is this?

- How does alphabetical order work exactly? What if two words begin with the same letter?

- Are there any other features on the page to help you find the right word, and how do they work? (Look at the top, sides and bottom of the page.)

Focusing on a typical entry

- What features are included in a typical entry and why?

- What order are these features in, and are there good reasons for this order?

- Are any presentational features used, e.g. different sizes, fonts, icons? Why?

⭐ 3 Planning the structure

It is now time to plan your writing. You need to consider how to structure your explanation and how to link your ideas clearly. This will help the reader follow the explanation and help you express it.

Use an explanation skeleton like the one begun below to help sketch out a plan.

As you can see, this skeleton includes an introduction and a conclusion. It also organises the material to match the research that you did, although you may want to vary the order.

Complete the skeleton by filling in the memory joggers.

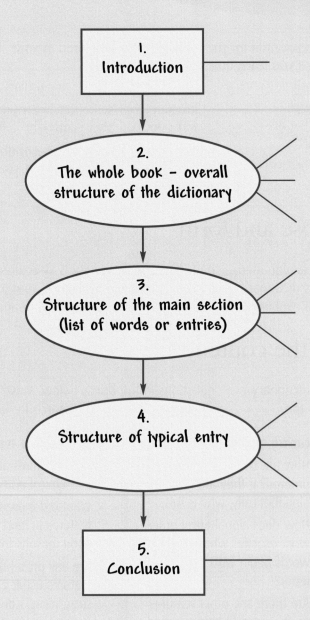

The Art of Explanation Writing

4 Composing your piece

 Once you have organised your ideas, decide how you are going to compose your piece both to interest your reader and provide a clear explanation.

Points to remember

As you write, remember to:

- use topic sentences early in each paragraph to make it clear what you are writing about (see page 50)
- write clearly, using plain and simple sentences, when you are explaining difficult ideas (see page 54)
- use metaphors and similes where appropriate to make the explanation more lively and accessible (see page 55)
- signpost the process by repeating key words, or by setting the scene (see page 56)
- use formal and impersonal language for the technical explanations, but be aware of the audience, so keep the language friendly and accessible
- highlight the cause and effect links by using different kinds of signposting (see page 58)
- use punctuation to make your meaning clear to the reader, focusing especially on commas around relative clauses where they add information and on avoiding the comma splice (see pages 59–60).

You may want to use some of the sentence signposts and connectives below to help you.

> **Sentence signposts and connectives**
> - This is because
> - The reason why
> - This is how alphabetical order
> - If all the text were the same size, then
> - So
> - It is very easy to take a dictionary for granted, because
> - For example
> - Let's now focus on
> - Because
> - Another reason for
> - Putting the 'guide for use' at the front

5 Peer comment

 Swap your draft with your partner's. Discuss together what really works well and highlight this on the draft. Now discuss what needs to be done to improve your explanations and jot down up to three suggestions on the draft.

Redraft the selected sections using these comments to guide you.

6 Pulling it all together

 Listen to some of the explanations written by members of the class.

 Decide what are the key features that make these extracts effective.

Be prepared to feed back your ideas.

Set up to three targets for yourself for improving your next piece of explanation writing.

E The Art of Instruction Writing

How instruction text works

AIMS

- Revisit the key ingredients of an instruction text.
- Use a text skeleton to analyse the structure of an instruction text.

In this section you will build on your existing knowledge of how instruction texts work, thinking about their audience, purpose and form, and focusing on their structure and language features.

Audience, purpose and form

Instruction texts tell you how to do something. Some examples are:

- **cake recipes**, such as those you have to follow in your D&T lesson
- **instruction manuals**, such as *The Book of Bike Maintenance*
- **handouts**, such as those from your ICT teacher telling you how to send an email.

You will hear instructions in every lesson, read them in most lessons and write them in English, D&T and Science lessons, among others.

TYPICAL FEATURES

The typical features of instruction text are listed below. You will need to refer to these in Section 2.

- The **audience** is someone who wants to know how to do something.
- Its **purpose** is to tell someone clearly how to do something.
- The **form** or structure of the text type is a series of step-by-step instructions describing how you do something. In particular, it is written in chronological order; the layout is designed to make instructions easy to follow, e.g. clear design, visual aids; a list format (bullets points, numbers) often makes the sequence clear; and diagrams are often used instead of description.

Typical **language features** of instruction texts are:

- simple, clear, brief, formal English, e.g. 'The waveband selected will appear in the display'
- technical language where necessary, e.g. 'On FM fully extend'
- use of the imperative,[1] e.g. 'Press the *On/Off* button'
- direct address (using the second person 'you'), e.g. 'Switch on your radio'
- time connectives (unless a numbered sequence), e.g. 'First set the time to zero...'.

---

[1] **imperative** – a verb in the imperative is one that gives orders, such as 'Go away!' or 'Be quiet!' Imperatives are also known as commands or directives.

The first half of the instruction text below has been annotated to illustrate some of the language features of an information text. Annotate the second half to provide another example of as many of these features as possible and note their effects.

How has the writer linked the diagrams in with the text? Is this successful?

Imperative verb – begins the instruction

List format – numbers show clear sequence to be followed

Short, clear sentence – helps the reader

Technical language – where necessary

Clear title – explains what instructions are about

Direct address to reader – second person 'your'

Operating Your Radio – Manual Tuning

1. <u>Switch</u> on your radio by pressing the *On/Off button*.

2. Select the required waveband by pressing the *Band button*. <u>The waveband selected will appear in the display.</u> On FM fully extend the *Telescopic aerial*. On MW and LW rotate <u>your</u> radio for best reception.

3. Press and release the *Tuning Up* or *Tuning Down button* or turn and release the *Tuning control* to change the frequency up or down.

4. Adjust the *Volume, Bass and Treble controls* to the required settings.

5. Press the *On/Off button* to switch off your radio.

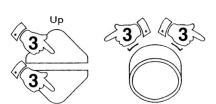

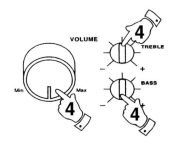

Using text skeletons

In order to understand the structure of a text, it can be useful to draw a diagram or 'text skeleton'. Text skeletons represent the bare bones of a text.

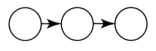

A typical instruction skeleton is given below. Each bubble represents one step in the sequence of instructions. In this case there is one bubble for each of the five numbered points in the text. Each bubble, or main point, follows on from the previous one, which is why the instruction skeleton is the same as the explanation skeleton. (However, in instruction text the sequence is a simple chronological one, which isn't always the case in explanation text.)

The notes in each bubble summarise the main thing that the reader is told to do at each step, for example 'Switch on'. The lines branching from each bubble are its key related points, or memory joggers, for example, 'Press *On/Off* button'.

Using text skeletons will help you to analyse the structure of a text and to plan your own writing.

Task 2 **Structuring**

Below is a partially-completed instruction text skeleton for *Operating Your Radio – Manual Tuning*. Discuss the main points and memory joggers you would add to bubbles 3, 4 and 5 to complete the skeleton.

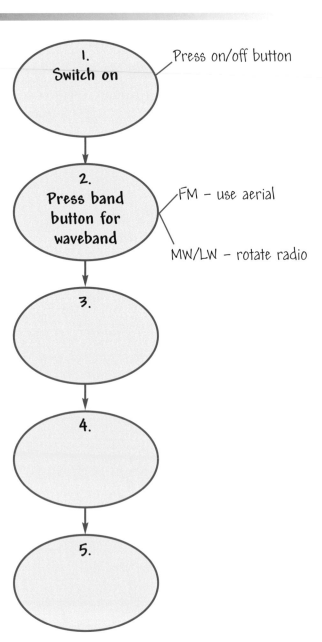

The Art of Instruction Writing

Composition and effect

Learning from example

AIMS

- Analyse and compare two texts to identify how well they provide instructions and how their effect depends on the language, viewpoint and presentation.

- Understand some of the differences between Standard English and non-Standard English.

In this section you will look at two versions of an instruction text and explain why one is better than the other. You will also investigate some of the differences between Standard English and non-Standard English.

Test watch As well as building up your writing skills, the following sections are good preparation for the optional reading tests at the end of Year 8 because they help you:

- comment on a writer's purpose and the effects of the text on the reader
- comment on the structure and organisation of texts
- comment on writers' use of language
- deduce, infer or interpret information, events or ideas
- describe, select or retrieve information, events or ideas from texts

If you show these skills in the reading test, you will gain a better mark.

Writing effective instructions

Writing effective instructions depends on thinking about the audience and purpose of the instructions, then choosing the right ingredients to make the instructions clear.

Task 3 Analysing

Sharon is writing a book about codes and coded messages for young people.

Her first draft and final version of the section on the square code is on page 68.

- Decide how you would annotate these versions to show why Sharon altered her first draft to produce the final version.

- Refer back to the panel of features for instruction texts on page 64.

- Then decide which features of the first draft do not make good instruction writing, and how the final version improves on this.

The Art of Instruction Writing

It may help to draw up a grid to compare the versions, like the one below.
Organise your comments in the following categories:

1. Choice of words

2. Choice of sentence length/type

3. Viewpoint of writer

4. Organisation/presentation of material

A few examples have been given below.

First draft	Final version	Why writer altered text
1. Choice of words 'really easy when you know how'	Not used	Unnecessary padding
'your special secret message'	'your message'	Don't need the adjectives
2. Choice of sentence length/type 'I've used the square code a lot '	Much shorter first sentence, and definition of rows and columns is put in a separate box	Clearer sentence so reader knows what the instruction is about from the start

FIRST DRAFT

Square Code

I've used the square code a lot – it's really easy when you know how, although you can get confused between rows and columns so remember that rows are horizontal and columns are vertical (I can't think of no easy way to remember this, sorry). A grid square makes your special secret message difficult for others to read.

To write your special secret message using the square code, I suggest you start by writing it horizontally (that's left to right) into the rows of a grid square. A good example of this is the following: MEET ME AT 3, when it is written horizontally, looks like this:
M E E
T M E
A T 3

Step 2. If you writes out the letters in each column as if they were words, you'll get what looks like complete gobbledegook:
MTA EMT EE3
Don't forget to separate each column by a space. You'll see why later.

Someone sent me this secret message written in the square code: ITOI CGUL AETL NTT4. How did I read it? I simply reversed the process. I wrote the coded message vertically into the columns of a grid square so that it look like this:
I C A N
T G E T
O U T T
I L L 4
(Why are the letters in the grid square above grouped in 4s? Well, look at how the letters in the secret message are grouped – geddit?) The message can now be read in the rows of your fabulous, magic square: I CANT GET OUT TILL 4.

How to Use the Square Code

In the square code you use the rows and columns of a grid square to make your message difficult for others to read.

Remember that a *row* is horizontal (it goes across from left to right)

To write a secret message using the square code, you must write it *horizontally* into the rows of a grid square. For example, MEET ME AT 3 becomes:

M	E	E
T	M	E
A	T	3

Then write out the letters in each column as if they were words, separating each column by a space. This gives you the coded message: MTA EMT EE3.

To decipher a secret message written this way, simply reverse the process. Imagine that this message came back to you:
ITOI CGUL AETL NTT4.

Write the coded message *vertically* into the columns of a grid square. The letters in the message above are grouped in 4s, which tells you that the columns must be 4 letters high:

I	C	A	N
T	G	E	T
O	U	T	T
I	L	L	4

Now you can read the message in the rows of the square:
I CANT GET OUT TILL 4.

Standard English – some rules

Sharon wrote her first draft quickly so she did not use Standard English in places:

1. *If you writes out*
2. *I can't think of no easy way to remember this.*

GRAMMAR

Standard English is the type of spoken and written English which pays close attention to the rules of grammar. It is the English dialect that is used by most English speakers and writers throughout the world. Three important rules of Standard English are:

1. The subject and verb of the sentence must agree, e.g. 'I write', 'you write'.
2. Verbs must have their past tense endings when you are speaking or writing about the past, e.g. 'I said', 'you spoke', 's/he looked'.
3. Two negatives should not be used within a sentence, e.g. 'We never did anything', not 'We never did nothing'.

Text structure and organisation

Getting the structure right

AIMS

- Make notes in different ways, choosing a form which suits the purpose.

- Analyse the overall structure of a text to identify how key ideas are developed.

- Describe a process clearly, linking sentences and clauses with connectives to signal each stage in the process.

In this section you will use a text skeleton to help you analyse the structure of the instruction text on codes, and think about what helps the reader understand the stages in the process.

Creating a text skeleton

Text skeletons sum up the structure of a text in a visual way (see page 66). The skeleton for instruction text helps you to understand the structure of *How to Use the Square Code* on page 69.

Task 4 **Notetaking**

Look at the text skeleton for the beginning of the final draft below. Complete the skeleton for the rest of the passage. Identifying the topic sentences[1] will help you.

> [1] **topic sentence (or key sentence)** – the sentence in a paragraph that signposts the focus of the paragraph. The topic sentence is often the first sentence of the paragraph.

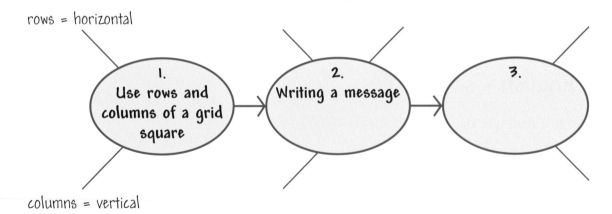

rows = horizontal

1. Use rows and columns of a grid square

2. Writing a message

3.

columns = vertical

Time connectives

Look at these two extracts from the *Square Code* instructions on page 69:

- *Then* write out the letters
- *Now* you can read the message

The words highlighted in mauve are time connectives. They make it clear to the reader that he or she has reached another stage in the instruction.

The panel lists some more time connectives. They are generally used to start sentences, as this makes the organisation of the text clear for the reader, but they can also be used to connect clauses within sentences.

Time connectives

- To begin with
- First
- Second
- Third
- Then

- Next
- At first
- When
- After

- Later on
- Until
- Eventually
- Finally

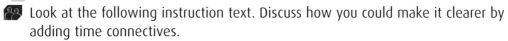

Task 5 **Discussing**

 Look at the following instruction text. Discuss how you could make it clearer by adding time connectives.

- Which time connectives would you add, and where?
- Do you need a time connective in each sentence? If not, why not?
- How else could you restructure the text to make it clearer?

Replacing your ink cartridge

Open the printer cover. Lift out the old cartridge and dispose of it. Remove the new cartridge from its package. Peel off the yellow seal. Place the ink cartridge into the cartridge holder. Push the clamp down until it locks firmly into place. Run a printing cycle. Your cartridge is ready

Numbered lists versus time connectives

Some instruction texts make the sequence of events in the process clear by using numbered lists. Other instructions, however, prefer to use continuous text with time connectives, which help to guide the reader.

Task 6 **Analysing**

Read the start of the two recipes for *Toad in the Hole* below. The first has used a numbered list, the second time connectives. Discuss why a writer should choose one method over the other. What are the advantages and disadvantages of each?

Toad in the Hole

1. Mix the batter ingredients together and put to one side.
2. Put 1cm of sunflower oil into a baking tin.
3. Place this on the middle shelf of your oven at 240°C.
4. When the oil is very hot, add the sausages.

Toad in the Hole

First you have to mix the batter ingredients together and put to one side.

While it is sitting there, put 1cm of sunflower oil into a baking tin. Then place this on the middle shelf of your oven at 240°C. When the oil is very hot, add the sausages.

The Art of Instruction Writing

2. Then you have to key in the number that you want to store, and you can make this as long as you want as long as it has 21 digits maximum because there's no room for more than that.

3. As you press each key, you can check you get it right because each number comes up on the display as you key it in.

4. At the end of all this, press the MEMORY key again and – hey presto – there's a beep and the display goes blank to show that the number you have just keyed in has now been stored in the memory.

Swap your rewritten instructions with a partner's and discuss who has made them clearer and more concise.

Colons and semicolons

GRAMMAR

The **colon** is a punctuation mark with three main uses:

1. To introduce a list, e.g. *You will need the following tools: a hammer, six nails, some string and a wooden baton.*

2. To introduce an example or quotation, e.g. *This gives you the coded message: MTA EMT EE3.*

3. To introduce a second clause that expands on, explains or illustrates the first, e.g. *He ought to look happy: he's just won the lottery.*

The **semicolon** has two main uses:

1. To separate lengthy items in a list, e.g. *You will need the following tools: a heavy hammer; six 3-inch nails; a length of string; and a wooden baton.*

2. To separate two clauses, each of which could stand on its own, e.g. *He's a very successful businessman; he's also just won the lottery.*

The key difference between them is that colons join and semicolons separate.

Task 10 **Discussing**

Scan the final version of the instruction text on codes (see page 69) and identify any colons and semicolons. Discuss these questions:

- What purpose does the colon have in each case?
- Would you expect to find semicolons in an instruction text? If not, why not?

Subordinate clauses and commas

Task 11 ## Discussing

 Look at the following two sentences. Each includes a subordinate clause of purpose, introduced by the word 'to'. What is different about the structure and punctuation of the sentences?

- *In the square code you use the rows and columns of a grid square to make your message difficult for others to read.*

- *To write a secret message using the square code, you must write it horizontally into the rows of a grid square.*

GRAMMAR

Punctuating complex sentences

1 When a subordinate clause begins a sentence, it should always be followed by a comma. This applies even if the clause is very short:
Exhausted, he fell to the ground.

2a When a subordinate clause follows the main clause, the comma is not generally used:
I will do it when I feel like it.

2b However, if the subordinate clause simply provides additional information or comment, you separate the clauses with a comma:
He lost the match, although it was very close.

Task 12 ## Writing

 Look at the main clause and the three subordinate clauses below. Your task is to combine them in six different ways to produce six grammatically correct sentences. Check that you have punctuated your sentences correctly. The first one has been done for you.

Main clause	Subordinate clauses
	If you are tired
You should go to bed now	Because you have a busy day tomorrow
	Although you can read until 9:30

1. If you are tired, you should go to bed now.

5 Composing your own instruction text

AIMS

- Plan, draft and present a text giving clear instructions to fit a particular audience and purpose.
- Reread and revise the work to anticipate the effect on the reader.

Your task

Write a set of clear instructions for a parent or carer to help them use their mobile phone to send text messages.

Test watch This writing task is good preparation for the type of writing required in your English tests because it helps you learn how to:

- plan your work so that it is organised logically into well-constructed paragraphs that are coherently linked together
- compose your writing effectively to match its audience and purpose,

- selecting appropriate vocabulary
- structure your sentences appropriately and punctuate them correctly.

If you show these skills in the optional English test at the end of Year 8, you will gain a better mark.

1 Audience and purpose

Your audience is an adult member of your family who has a mobile phone but who does not know how to use it to send text messages. Your task is to describe how it is done, in a series of sequenced steps.

2 Discussing

 Discuss what effect the audience and purpose of this task will have on the style of your instructions. In particular, consider these questions:

- Will your audience be familiar with

the specialist language of mobile phones?

- How formal should the language be?
- Are visual features, such as diagrams or different fonts, appropriate?

3 Working out the content

 You probably send text messages without thinking about it, but remember that your audience does not.

Brainstorm all the things that you do when you text a message and jot down notes about them.

4 Planning the structure

TR Text skeletons are very useful tools to help structure your writing.

Use an instruction skeleton, like the one below, to sum up the sequence of steps that your parent must take.

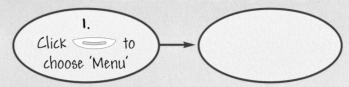

Composing your piece

 You are ready to draft your instructions.

Points to remember

As you write, remember to:
- begin each instruction with an imperative, or use 'you'
- use Standard English and language of an appropriate formality (see page 69)
- use technical language where necessary
- sequence your instructions chronologically (see page 71)
- keep your sentences short (see page 73)

- if you are not using numbered lists, make sure your topic sentences emphasise the sequence and use time connectives and patterned language (see page 70–71)
- consider how the presentation and/or diagrams could help to make the instructions clear
- make sure that your punctuation is clear and accurate (see page 75)
- use colons and semicolons (see page 74).

You may want to use some of the sentence signposts and connectives below to help.

Sentence signposts and connectives
- First
- Second
- When
- Then add
- Next
- Finally
- Now type

Peer comment

 Swap your draft with a partner's and read it carefully. Imagine that you know nothing about texting – are these instructions clear and useful? Look back at the list above, decide what really works well and highlight this on the draft. Discuss how you could improve your instructions and jot down three suggestions.

Then redraft the selected sections of your instructions, using your partner's comments to guide you.

Pulling it all together

 Listen to some of the instructions written by members of the class.

Decide what are the key features that make these extracts effective. Be prepared to feed back your ideas.

Set up to three targets for improving your next piece of instruction writing.

F The Art of Persuasive Writing

How persuasion text works

AIMS

Revisit the key ingredients of persuasion text, thinking about how it uses rhetorical devices.

Use text skeletons to help analyse the structure of persuasion text and make notes on its content.

In this section you will build on your existing knowledge of how persuasive writing works, thinking about its audience, purpose and form and focusing on its typical structure and language features.

Audience, purpose, form

Persuasive writing puts forward a particular view and tries to get the reader to agree with that view. Some typical examples are:

- **adverts**, which try to persuade you to buy something
- **political speeches**, which try to persuade you to vote for or against a proposal
- **newspaper editorials**, which try to persuade you to agree with their point of view.

You will use this type of writing particularly in English and History, and aspects of D&T.

TYPICAL FEATURES

The typical features of persuasion texts are listed below. You will need to refer to these in Section 2.

- The **audience** is someone you are trying to influence.
- The **purpose** is to change their view or to persuade them to do something.
- The **form** or structure of persuasion text often includes a series of points in a logical order, supporting a single viewpoint; topic sentences to introduce each point; visuals such as slogans or images to reinforce the key points.

Typical **language features** of persuasion texts are:

- emotive[1] language, e.g. '**Enjoy** 3x faster Tiscali Broadband'
- personal pronouns, e.g. 'every time you want to use'
- inclusive phrases or connectives to encourage the reader to want something, e.g. 'which means you and your family'
- friendly tone – almost as if talking to you, e.g. 'so you can use the Internet as much as you want'.

[1] **emotive** – designed to make the audience feel something

The first half of the advert below has been annotated to illustrate the language and structural features of a persuasive text.

Read the text and the annotations carefully, then discuss how you would annotate the second half to show another example of as many of the features as you can.

Repetition – to drive home key points

Friendly tone

Personal pronouns – appealing directly to reader, 'you'

Inclusive phrase – chosen to encourage you to want the product

Topic heading – to emphasise key messages

Structure – series of points supporting one viewpoint

Emotive language – chosen to lure you into selecting their services

BROADBAND BENEFITS

What is Broadband?

Broadband is high speed, <u>always-on</u> Internet access. An <u>always-on</u> connection means that <u>you don't have to dial up every time you</u> want to use the Internet, you're permanently connected. Plus broadband keeps your phone line free <u>which means you and your family</u> can use the phone whilst you're online. With Tiscali Broadband there are no Internet call charges so you can use the Internet as much as you want, whenever you want, for one low flat monthly fee.

<u>Why should I choose Tiscali Broadband over AOL or Freeserve?</u>

Quite simply because we offer an excellent quality broadband service and a wide choice of packages at some of the most affordable prices in the UK! <u>Enjoy</u> 3X faster Tiscali Broadband at just £15.99 a month (that's the same price as AOL standard dial-up) or choose 10X faster Tiscali Broadband at just £24.99 a month. Both products come with a free modem and completely free set-up! Tiscali combines all the benefits of broadband with easy installation and a dedicated customer support team.

Why is Broadband better than standard dial up?

1. It's faster

Enjoy Internet access up to 10 times faster than a standard 56kbps dial-up connection.

2. It's always on

There's no need to wait to get online. You're permanently connected until you turn your PC off.

3. It keeps your phone line free

Surf the Internet and talk on the phone at the same time.

4. It's easy to install

There is no need to call an engineer. Once you've registered we'll send you your broadband modem with simple instructions on how to set this up on your PC.

5. It's a new experience

Tiscali Broadband changes the way you use the Internet. You can shop and bank online, instantly download music and games in seconds, email large attachments easily, watch music and film clips from your PC, and much more!

new members
join now >>

existing members
upgrade now >>

 The headings act as topic sentences, introducing the focus of each section. What is the effect of using these headings? Be prepared to share your conclusions.

The Art of Persuasive Writing

Using text skeletons

In order to understand the structure of a text, it can be useful to draw a diagram or 'text skeleton'. Text skeletons represent the bare bones of a text.

The typical persuasion skeleton shows a series of main points listed down the page in a logical order, indicated by asterisks (✳). Each main point often has a paragraph to itself in the text. The labels to the left of the asterisks tell you the focus of each paragraph, for example, 'What is Broadband?'. These labels are usually a shortened version of the topic sentence. The lines branching to the right from each asterisk summarise statements (memory joggers) that back up or expand the main point, for example 'keeps phone line free'.

Using text skeletons will help you to analyse the structure of a text and plan your own writing.

Task 3 | Structuring

Below is a half-completed text skeleton for the advert *Broadband Benefits*.
Complete the skeleton and memory joggers so that you have a full set of notes on the text. You will need to add three more bubbles to cover points 3 to 5.

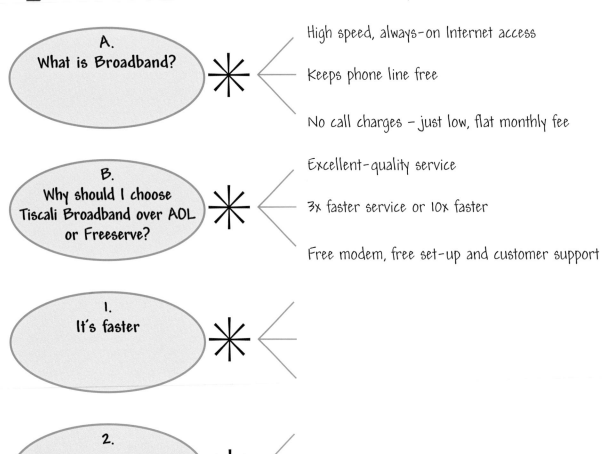

Learning from example

AIMS

- Adapt the stylistic conventions of persuasion text to fit different audiences, purposes and media.

- Present a case persuasively, using appropriate rhetorical devices and anticipating responses and objections.

- Use different degrees of formality to suit audience and purpose, recognising how this influences word choice.

In this section you will read a persuasion text and explore how it is effective. You will identify and discuss its key features, focusing on how it addresses the audience and on the writer's choice of words and rhetorical devices.[1]

> [1] **rhetorical devices** – techniques used to persuade an audience, such as alliteration, emotive language and rhetorical questions (e.g. 'anywhere and anytime') (e.g. 'Is there anyone who still thinks that…?')

Test watch As well as building up your writing skills, the following sections are good preparation for the optional reading tests at the end of Year 8 because they help you to:

- comment on a writer's purpose and the effects of the text on the reader
- comment on the structure and organisation of texts
- comment on a writer's use of language
- deduce, infer or interpret information, events or ideas
- describe, select or retrieve information, events or ideas from texts.

If you show these skills in the reading test, you will gain a better mark.

Audience and purpose

Task 4 Analysing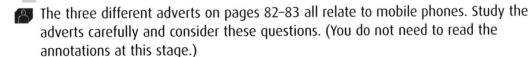

The three different adverts on pages 82–83 all relate to mobile phones. Study the adverts carefully and consider these questions. (You do not need to read the annotations at this stage.)

- What sort of audience do you think each advert is aimed at? Consider each audience's age, gender and whether they are mobile phone users or not.
- How does the amount of text used in each advert reflect its audience and purpose?

Be prepared to feed back your views, with evidence to support your answers.

The Art of Persuasive Writing

Emotive language

Personal pronouns – ('you'/'your') appeal directly to the reader

Technical name – makes product sound effective

Headings/ slogans – emphasise key messages

And it's not just QuickShare™ that puts the T610 in front...

It sounds great
Compose your own 32-bit polyphonic ring tones using the T610's ringtone composer. Plus assign ring tones and sounds to contacts in your address book, along with pictures so you can both see and hear who's calling.

It's great fun
Superb graphics, excellent sound effects and a joystick control combine to make the T610 the perfect mobile gaming companion. There are extra games available to download via Entertainment on the T610 menu.

It can be serious when it wants to be
Diary, Contacts, To Do list - they're all in there, despite the T610's small size. Plus there's email, Bluetooth™, GPRS and PC synchronisation software - everything a serious business person needs on the move.

It looks great
But state of the art technology aside, let's not forget that good, old fashioned view of the importance of good looks. And there's no doubt that with its black and aluminium finish and small, slim size, the T610 has no worries in that area.

Emotive language

Structure – a series of points supporting one viewpoint

Repetition – drives home key point

Clever use of language – associates good looks with tradition

Association of ideas – these intend a would-be purchaser to think that if they buy this phone they will be seen as a real business person as well as 'cool'

Advert 2

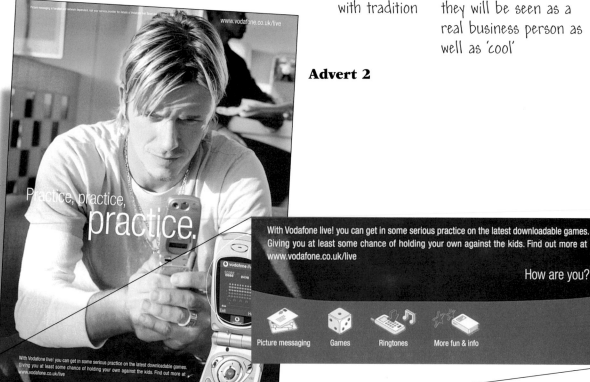

Advert 3

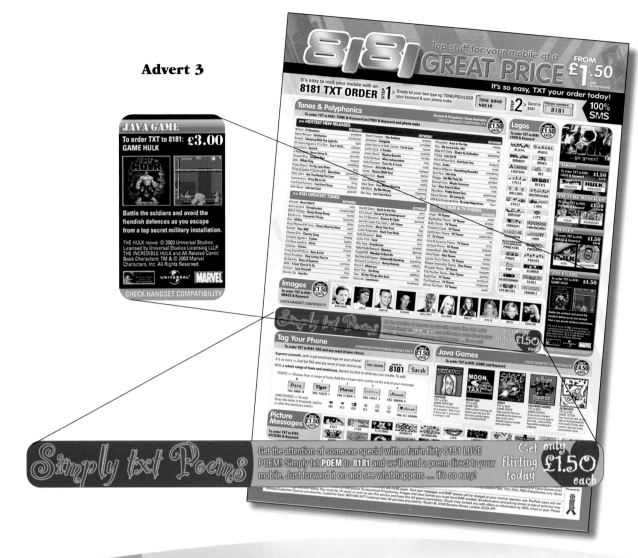

Persuasive language and advertising

TYPICAL FEATURES

- **slogan** – a key message which acts as a headline for the advert, e.g. 'Find out fast'

- **technical/scientific language** – this is intended to make the product seem convincing, e.g. 'contains DO5'

- **clever use of language** (including wordplay, rhyme, alliteration slogans or invented words) to attract attention, e.g. 'Beanz meanz Heinz'

- **brand names, logos and particular colours** which become associated with the product, e.g. **NIKE** ✓

- **association of ideas** – words or images linking your product with something that you think your audience will want, like a glamorous lifestyle, e.g. 'Because you're worth it' by L'Oreal. L'Oreal models always look at the peak of health and beauty. The advertisers hope their audience will think they could look that good if only they bought the product.

Task 5 **Annotating**

Annotate Advert 2 on page 82 to illustrate as many of these additional features as possible, as well as the typical features of persuasive text (see page 82). Use the annotations on Advert 1 to guide you. Be prepared to feed back your conclusions.

Powerful slogans to attract the reader

The most important text in any advert is the slogan – the headline text that attempts to grab the audience's attention. Copywriters will spend hours brainstorming ideas to establish a suitable slogan, like the three below.

Slogans, like headline writing, require special language skills. A slogan should:

- sum up the key message of the advert
- suit the audience at which the advert is aimed.

Slogans are usually:

- active and immediate
- short, snappy and informal
- memorable (often including wit and/or effects like alliteration, rhyme or repetition).

 Task 6 | **Presenting**

> You are working for an advertising agency that specialises in mobile phone advertisements. You have just devised the three slogans shown above. Your task now is to present your slogans to the campaign director.
>
> Prepare your presentation. Refer back to the features of slogans above to explain how each slogan fits the audience for which it has been devised.

Inclusive phrases to involve the reader

Inclusive sentence signposts, which invite you to join in or suggest everyone thinks or behaves in a certain way, are a key rhetorical device for persuasive writing.

Discursive signposts tend to have the opposite aim, i.e. to suggest there are at least two sides to the argument. In the grid on page 85 one signpost in each column has been misplaced.

Task 7 | **Categorising**

> Look carefully at the table on page 85. Identify the four misplaced signposts and work out which column they should be in. (Remember, three of the four signposts in each column are in the correct place.)

The Art of Persuasive Writing

Signposts to make people agree with you (persuasive)	Signposts to make people take the opposite viewpoint (persuasive)	Signposts that invite the reader to join in (persuasive)	Signposts to suggest that it is a complex issue (discursive)
1. A child of three could...	2. This is just the sort of appalling...	3. Picture yourself wearing...	4. Who would now argue that...
5. For decades it's been recognised that...	6. Are you willing to stand there and...	7. All decent-minded people will...	8. The best way forward is hard to determine because...
9. It must be clear by now that...	10. This is a complex issue because...	11. Hurry, offer ends ...	12. The path of righteousness is not always clear because...
13. Now you too can...	14. No sensible person could possibly...	15. Ring today to...	16. Complex problems defy easy answers...

Level of formality

Look at this statement: **"The language of persuasion is never very formal or impersonal."**

- Discuss whether this statement is true. Be prepared to support your answer.

Task 8 **Selecting**

  Below are extracts from the three adverts ranging in formality, depending on their audience and purpose. (See page 41 for more on formal and informal texts.)

- Number the extracts beginning with the least formal (1) and ending with the most formal (4). Be prepared to present your order, giving reasons for your choice.

  You could begin your explanation like this:

  We decided that extract X was the least formal because...

A

Battle the soldiers and avoid the fiendish defences as you escape from a top secret military installation.

B

C

And it's not just QuickShare™ that puts the T610 in front...

D

Giving you at least some chance of holding your own against the kids.
www.vodafone.co.uk/live

The advertising challenge

Task 9 **Writing**

 Your company is about to bring out a new brand of washing powder. The three possible names proposed are **BRILL**, **AGENT 32** or **CLEAN**.

- Decide who the audience is for your product and select the name that you think will be the most effective. If you don't like any of the suggestions, think of your own brand name.
- Then work out a slogan to help launch the powder. (Look back at page 84 for help.)

Getting the structure right

AIMS

- Make notes choosing a form which suits their purpose.
- Analyse the overall structure of a text to identify how key ideas are developed.

Creating a text skeleton

Text skeletons sum up the structure of a text in a visual way (see page 80). The skeleton for a persuasion text will help you understand the structure of the T610 advert on page 82.

Task 10 **Structuring**

Look at the text skeleton for the beginning of the Orange T610 advert below and complete the skeleton for the rest of the extract (see page 82). Remember that the headings act as topic sentences (see page 79), so use them to help you.

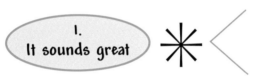

Compose own ring tones

Assign tones, sounds and pictures to contacts
Great for mobile games

Extra games available to download

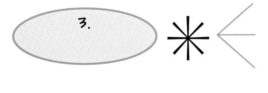

Signposting the text

Successful advertising helps companies stay in business. The advertisers for Orange decided they had four key points to make, and that putting them in the order above would make the most impact. Organising the points in separate paragraphs gives the text coherence[1].

However, these points also need to link together well. Part of the advertiser's task is to connect and develop a persuasive argument clearly. This contributes to the cohesion[2] of the text.

[1] **cohesion** – how individual sections of text hang together and relate to the sections around them. References back, contrasts, connectives and sentence signposts are some of the signals that make a text cohesive.

[2] **coherence** – the overall consistency of a text, or how it hangs together as a whole. Organising your ideas by using paragraphs, subheadings, layout conventions and presentational devices makes a text coherent.

 Task 11 **Analysing cohesion**

 Reread the Orange T610 advert.

> And it's not just QuickShare™ that puts the T610 in front…
>
> **It sounds great**
> Compose your own 32-bit polyphonic ring tones using the T610's ringtone composer. Plus assign ring tones and sounds to contacts in your address book, along with pictures so you can both see and hear who's calling.
>
> **It's great fun**
> Superb graphics, excellent sound effects and a joystick control combine to make the T610 the perfect mobile gaming companion. There are extra games available to download via Entertainment on the T610 menu.

Refers back to the first paragraph's focus on sound

Identify the phrases or clauses that link these two paragraphs and complete the annotations begun above. Remember, a link can be achieved by contrast as well as similarity. Be prepared to present your ideas.

Understanding the power of images

Many adverts rely on large visual images, as well as words, to get their message across. The images and words have to hang together just like text does in Advert 1.

Task 12 **Analysing**

 The Vodafone live! advert on page 82 is made up of the following elements.

Slogan across centre of advert: 'Practice, practice, practice'.

Short paragraph in small font

The question 'How are you?' near the bottom of page

Out-of-focus hi-tech background

Large close up of David Beckham using Vodafone live! software on his mobile

Close up of open mobile so you can view the game being played

Red banner at bottom of advert containing Vodafone's logo and four icons related to the functions of the mobile phone

Analyse how the Vodafone live! advert hangs together.

- Which elements are largest or given the most space? Why is this?
- How are the elements laid out to convince the reader to buy this phone?

The teen mobile

Planning practice

You are employed by a mobile phone company, which is interested in attracting 13- to 15-year-olds. Your task is to plan an outline for a four-paragraph advertising leaflet, including images. The company has supplied you with seven ideas, although if you have better ideas, use them instead.

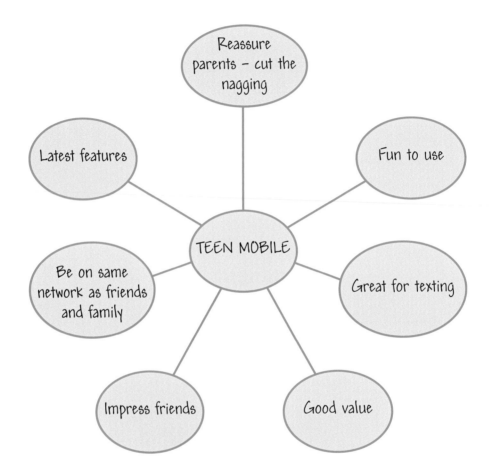

Select your key selling point (the most powerful point) and plan a design for a leaflet including:

- the order you would put the points in
- the type of images you will use
- the colour scheme
- the slogan – related to the key selling point.

Making the sentences work

AIMS

- Explore the impact of a variety of sentence structures, recognising when it is effective to use minor sentences.

In this section you will focus on the impact of minor sentences to create particular effects. Then you will craft lively sentences that pack in information.

Using minor sentences

GRAMMAR

Formal English is written in **complete sentences** (sometimes referred to as **major sentences**), which make sense on their own. They contain a complete verb, which is technically known as a finite verb. For example:

The dog **chased** the cat.

Having checked that no traffic was coming, he **crossed** the road.

Run!

Minor sentences (sometimes called **special sentences**) do not have a complete (finite) verb. Instead, they make sense because of their context (the sentences or circumstances that surround them). They are often used as headings, on signs, in adverts and in conversations. Many story writers use them to add interest to their writing because they are often very short and 'hard-hitting'. For example:

- Whatever.
- No parking!
- Sale!
- Sure thing.
- Rain. Endless rain. No going out today.

Task 14 | **Discussing**

The minor sentences have been underlined in the two extracts below. Both extracts have also been rewritten in standard sentences.

From Advert 2

With Vodafone live! you can get in some serious practice on the latest downloadable games. Giving you at least some chance of holding your own against the kids.

With Vodafone live! you can get in some serious practice on the latest downloadable games. **This gives you at least some chance of holding your own against the kids.**

From Advert 3

only £1.50 each

They are only £1.50 each.

Why are minor sentences more effective here than standard sentences would have been? Be prepared to feed back your response.

The Art of Persuasive Writing

Respinning sentences

You need to consider the audience of your sentences when deciding whether they should be simple or complex. Using the 'right' kind of sentence will make it much more effective.

Task 15 **Redrafting**

  Rewrite this complex sentence taken from Advert 3 in at least two different ways. You can add or leave out words but the sense must remain the same. Try to come up with sentences that have more impact than the original. For example:

> Battle the soldiers and avoid the fiendish defences as you escape from a top secret military installation.

You could try using these words to begin your sentences:

You...   Escape...

> Avoid the fiendish defences and battle the soldiers while escaping from a top secret military installation.

Be prepared to present your sentences along with the original, explaining which is the best.

Punctuating sentences correctly

If you don't punctuate your writing properly, the reader is likely to misunderstand your meaning.

GRAMMAR

Full stop .	Ends a sentence
Colon :	Marks a strong pause and used in lists
Semicolon ;	Indicates a stronger pause than a comma
Brackets ( )	Separates items in a list
Comma ,	Separates words, phrases or clauses that provide extra information; indicates pauses
Hyphen -	Shows that a word continues on the next line; links words to make a compound word or phrases to make an adjective.
Dash –	Shows a short pause, or separates out information in a sentence
Elipsis ...	Shows missing text
Question mark ?	Indicates a question
Apostrophe '	Indicates possession or a missing letter(s)
Exclamation mark !	Indicates an exclamation or command
Speech marks " "	Shows direct speech or quotations

Task 16 **Analysing**

Look at the extract from T610 below and explain the purpose of all the punctuation and capitalisation.

> Diary, Contacts, To Do list – they're all in there, despite the T610's small size. Plus there's email, BluetoothTM, GPRS and PC synchronisation software – everything a serious business person needs on the move.

The writer could have used colons instead of the dashes. Why do you think dashes were chosen?

5 Composing a persuasive letter

AIMS

- Present a case persuasively, adapting the conventions of persuasion text to fit a particular audience and purpose, and use appropriate rhetorical devices.

- Develop and signpost the argument, making the connections clear.

- Use the appropriate degrees of formality to suit audience and purpose, recognising how this influences word choice.

Your task

Write an advertising leaflet clearly targeted at its audience.

Test watch This writing task is good preparation for the type of writing required in your English tests because it helps you learn how to:

plan your work so that it is organised logically into well-constructed paragraphs that are linked together well

compose your writing effectively to match its audience and purpose,

and select powerful vocabulary

vary the structure of your sentences and punctuate them correctly.

If you show these skills in the optional English test at the end of Year 8, you will gain a better mark.

---

1 Audience and purpose

Your task is to write a short advertising leaflet to persuade adults who do not own a mobile phone to buy one. You need to persuade them to buy a brand of phone called **Connect**. You should also suggest an accompanying image.

Discuss the effect the audience and purpose of this advert will have on its style.

Will your audience be familiar with the terminology used about mobile phones?

What association of ideas will be the most effective? What feelings do you want connected with your product? (Is it cool? Is it practical?)

Which emotions do you want to raise? (Guilt? Happiness? Relaxation?)

2 Brainstorming the content

Brainstorm all the arguments that could persuade your audience. Remember, these adults have probably never bought a mobile phone because:

they don't want to be bothered all the time

they find the noise and people's use of the phones irritating

they worry about the cost

they have heard they might be a health hazard.

Some ideas have been begun for you.

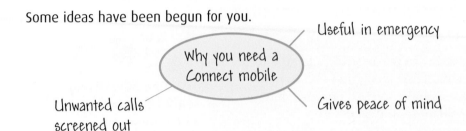

Tick the three or four most important points. Then list the negative points you wish to counter.

3 Planning the structure

List the points you have selected above in the most persuasive order.

Complete your persuasion skeleton by jotting down ideas to support each key point.

Decide on a slogan to be the hook for the advert. (See page 84.)

4 Discussing what you are going to write

Take it in turns to present your leaflet plan to your partner. When you are not presenting, listen carefully and be prepared to offer advice on how to develop or add detail to the leaflet. Your role is to make suggestions to help your partner. Adapt your plan, if appropriate, in the light of this discussion.

5 Composing your piece

Now you are ready to start drafting your persuasive leaflet.

Points to remember

As you write, remember to:

- decide how to word your slogan for maximum effect (see page 84)
- use headings/topic sentences/ images to help the reader grasp the key messages easily (see pages 79 and 87)
- select a friendly tone (see page 85)
- use a powerful opening paragraph (see pages 86–87)

- use sentence signposts and connectives to join your ideas together to maximise the power of your argument (see page 86)
- vary the length and type of your sentences, using both simple or minor sentences for impact (see page 89)
- involve your reader by using inclusive phrases and connectives (see page 84)
- use emotive language and clever phrases (see page 83).

You may want to use some of the sentence signposts and connectives below.

Sentence signposts and connectives

- Just imagine
- It's at a time like this
- For those moments you can't plan for
- You don't have to
- And it's not
- You probably dislike mobile phones because

- If only you'd had a
- And for those special moments
- but then
- Just turn it on when

6 Peer comment

 Swap your draft with your partner's and read each other's carefully. Discuss what works well and highlight this on the draft. Then discuss how you could improve particular sections. Jot down your suggestions on the draft.

Redraft your advertising leaflet, using your partner's comments to guide you.

7 Pulling it all together

Listen to some of the leaflets written by members of your class.

Discuss the key features that make these effective.

Set up to three targets for yourself for improving your next piece of persuasive writing.

G The Art of Presenting an Argument

How argument text works

AIMS

- Revisit the key ingredients of text that presents an argument.
- Use text skeletons to help analyse and structure opinion text.

In this section you will build on your knowledge of how to present an argument, focusing on audience, purpose and form.

Audience, purpose, form

Opinion texts use structured, logical argument to express a point of view. Examples are:

- **letters to newspapers**, such as those in response to an article
- **opinion essays**, such as those you may be asked to write in English, History or RE
- **newspaper and magazine articles**, that give the point of view of the writer.

Arguing a case is a particular kind of persuasion. Some of the features of persuasive writing (see page 78), such as rhetorical and emotive language, are less important in a reasoned argument text.

TYPICAL FEATURES

The typical features of argument or opinion text are listed in the panel below. You will need to refer to these in Section 2.

- The **audience** is someone you are trying to influence.
- The **purpose** is to get them to agree with your viewpoint.
- The **form** or structure of argument text often includes a title summing up the argument; an opening statement introducing the viewpoint; a series of main points backing this up (supported by evidence and comment); topic sentences introducing each main point; a conclusion summarising the argument.

Typical **language features** are:

- formal language avoiding colloquialisms,[1] e.g. 'The key point to remember is'
- use of the first, second or third person, depending on the audience and purpose. More formal opinion writing uses the third person, e.g. 'It can be argued' as opposed to 'I think that' or 'surely you can see'
- passive[2] sentences to add an impersonal tone, e.g. ' It could be argued that'
- reasonable and restrained tone – winning over the audience by reason rather than by using clever rhetorical techniques, e.g. 'If you think about this carefully'
- emotive language used sparingly to sway the audience, e.g. 'Surely any human being would feel'

[1] **colloquialism** – the kind of language used in conversation. Colloquial language often includes shortened forms of words and slang and dialect, e.g. 'If it ain't one thing, it's another'

[2] **passive** – the 'voice' used when the subject of a sentence is acted upon by the verb, e.g. 'The man was arrested.' Passive sentences tell you what happened and who or what it happened to, but they do not necessarily tell you who or what performed the action.

Annotating

Read the adaptation from a web rant below. One example of each of the language and structural features listed on page 94 has been annotated. Identify another example of as many of these ingredients as possible in the final two paragraphs.

Striking title summing up the opinion and grabbing attention

Topic sentence – introduces focus of paragraph

Series of points – supporting argument

Logical sentence signposts – guide the reader

Emotive language – attempt to get audience to agree with argument

Evidence – supports a main point

A PLAGUE ON TEXTING

Hi! ds bd grmmr annoy u? I am here for a rant, so don't expect a huge amount of balance.

The key thing that gets me about text messaging is how annoying the whole process is. When you're writing a message, you spend half an hour writing a sentence. I could write a novelette in the time it takes me to compose a text message. One-finger keying is very frustrating.

There are other reasons for wanting to ban text messaging. One that is high up the agenda is the whole daft concept of chatting via messages. If you've got a phone, why don't you use it? It's so much nicer to hear the voice of someone you know rather than just read a message. Not only that, but messages can be misconstrued when written, but when you're speaking it makes it so much easier to communicate what you really mean.

Do you need another reason to hate text messaging? People in education have been warning us, but no one seems to listen. Messaging is killing grammar. Because so many kids use text messages all the time, they've forgotten vowels exist.

The English language is better for the diversity and colloquial terms it has created and the way that it has evolved over the centuries, but such an unnatural form of writing like text messaging will kill all the beauty in the English language. In a world of consumerism, where people are under the impression that they have to rush to do everything, they have decided to cut out verbal communication too. Things have gone too far. Push up the price of texting, push up the price of phones or just burn every single one on the planet. Which is more important; the sanity of a minority or the insanity and illiteracy of the majority? Decide for yourself.

Informal language – suited to web medium

Questions directly addressed to reader to guide reader

Formal language – makes a serious point but directly addressing reader

Topic sentences

Discuss what you think the purpose of this text is. Now consider what the text is about. The best way of doing this is to look at the topic sentences. The first three have been highlighted in orange. Now identify the topic sentences in paragraphs 4 and 5.

Use these sentences to help you summarise the extract. Be prepared to present your summary.

The Art of Presenting an Argument

Using text skeletons

In order to understand the structure of a text, it can be useful to draw a diagram or 'text skeleton'. Text skeletons represent the bare bones of a text.

The structure of an argument text can be summed up by the persuade text skeleton (see page 80). The asterisks are the main points of the argument, e.g. 'Chatting via messaging is daft'. These are often a shortened form of the topic sentences. The supporting statements that back up or expand the main point, e.g. 'Why not speak on the phone?' are shown as lines from the asterisks and are known as memory joggers.

Using text skeletons will help you analyse the structure of a text, take notes on a text and plan your own writing.

Task 3 — **Structuring**

Below is the beginning of a text skeleton for the web rant article. Complete the skeleton so that you have a full set of main points and memory joggers for the text.

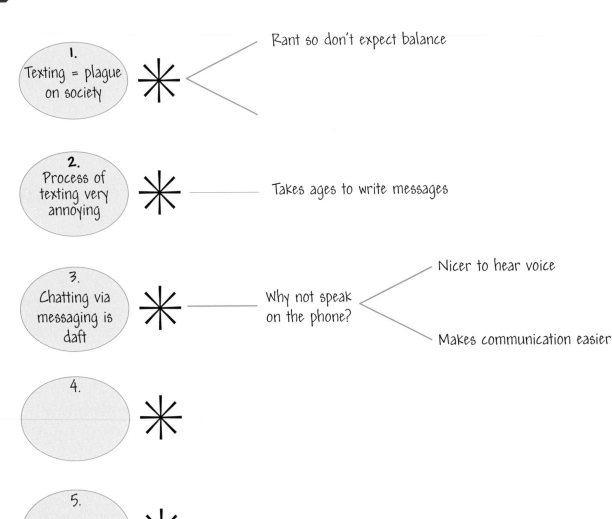

2 Composition and effect

AIMS

- Adapt the stylistic conventions of persuasion text to fit writing a letter on a controversial issue.

- Recognise bias and objectivity, distinguishing facts from theories and opinions.

- Examine how writers present their viewpoints persuasively, making selective use of evidence, using rhetorical devices, and anticipating responses and objections.

In this section you will analyse the stylistic techniques used in three emails that express strong opinions, and examine how the writers have expressed their ideas to win readers round to their way of thinking.

Test watch As well as building up your writing skills, the following sections are good preparation for the optional reading tests at the end of Year 8 because they help you:

- comment on a writer's purpose and the effects of the text on the reader

- comment on the structure and organisation of texts

- comment on a writers' use of language

- deduce, infer or interpret information, events or ideas

- describe, select or retrieve information, events or ideas from texts.

If you show these skills in the reading test, you will gain a better mark.

Opening up the debate

In 2003 the news was full of the story of a 12-year-old girl who ran away with a 32-year-old man whom she had met via an Internet chatroom. On page 98, there are three email letters written as a result of the debate that followed. They appeared in the debate column of a national newspaper.

Task 4 **Reading and analysing**

As you read the letters, consider:

- how the viewpoints differ

- how each writer has developed their arguments

- and what techniques they have used to try and win their readers round to their way of thinking.

The Art of Presenting an Argument

Interesting opening – helps hook the reader

Series of points – supporting argument

Emotive language – makes audience worry about what is happening

Logical connectives and sentence signposts – guide the reader through the text

Title – sums up point of argument

Direct address (second person) – used to take argument direct to parents

Topic sentence – introducing focus of paragraph

Passive tense – adds to formality

Evidence – supporting a main point

1.

<u>Chatroom Checks</u>

I AM a teen myself and it is very easy to log on to the Internet and go into chatrooms. In some rooms there are categories such as Romance; After Hours; Blind Date; Love Shack; and Rendezvous. <u>Kids are easily able to enter any of these rooms</u>

<u>So</u>, parents, are <u>you</u> absolutely sure that your child is chatting with other children they can trust, or are they really attracting <u>dangerous</u> strangers?

Please take my advice – <u>block these rooms if you can</u>, and if you can't, check to see who they are talking to.

(Teenage girl – name and address supplied)

2.

Program Safety

THE Internet is not a dangerous place. Millions of people access the Internet every day. The only reason it seems dangerous is that we only ever hear of it being misused by hackers, paedophiles and other criminals.

Using programs such as MSN Messenger, users talk only to people who know their email address. Parents should encourage their children to use programs like this and, if they must use less secure programs, to use them safely.

Lecturing and forbidding means only that the child is more likely to want to experience these forbidden delights.

(14-year-old boy)

3.

Virtually on the Streets

Before the advent of the Internet era, some parents used the television set as a makeshift babysitter. Kids were exposed to a multitude of violence fed to them through cartoons and television shows, and some acted out what they saw on television. We now have the Internet, which is being used in the same way.

I feel that parents should be as vigilant as possible when their children are on the Net, and that they should not be afraid to press the 'off' button on their computers.

I simply would not allow my children or grandchildren to use the Net by themselves for an hour, much less five or six hours a day. Letting them have free access to the web is the same as allowing them to hang out on the streets till all hours: they are prey to the same dangers online as they are on the streets.

Parents need to have more time for their children and play a more active role in their upbringing. If the child wants to use the Internet, go online with them for 30 minutes at a time, the same amount of time one would spend watching a television programme, and then move on to something else.

(Male writer – name and email address supplied)

Task 5 **Annotating**

 Letter 1 on page 98 has been annotated to illustrate the key features of opinion writing. Annotate letter 2 to illustrate as many of the argument text features as possible (see the panel on page 94). Be prepared to feed back your conclusions.

Anticipating responses and objections

If you want to convince someone about something, it is a good idea to think through any possible objections so that you can counter them in your argument.

Task 6 **Analysing**

Skim-read letter 2 to find evidence that the writer has come up with objections and argued against them. Be prepared to present your conclusions with evidence to back up your views. One example has been done for you:

Letter 2: Raises objection that Internet seems dangerous Explains that this is because only get to hear about hackers, paedophiles and other criminals

Presenting opinion as fact

When writers are making an argument, they often disguise their opinions[2] or theories[3] in the language of fact[1] to make them sound convincing.

[1] **fact** – an event or thing known to have happened or existed (warning: people often dress up opinion in the language of fact)

[2] **opinion** – judgement or belief not founded on certainty or proof

[3] **theory** – an idea that is put forward based on evidence, a possible solution to a problem; 'theory' is a non-technical word for 'hypothesis'

Below are nine sentence signposts that signal to the reader or listener that what follows is, supposedly, a theory, a fact or an opinion. The signposts in rows 1 and 2 are in the appropriate columns but the signposts in row 3 are not.

Task 7 **Categorising**

Work out whether the sentence signposts in the last row should have been placed under A, B or C.

	A. Fact	B. Opinion	C. Theory
1	Science has proved that	In my view	An alternative theory is
2	Research has consistently revealed	I've always believed that	The evidence can be interpreted differently
3	The worst thing about hunting is	It is worth considering	Forensic experts agree that

Selecting emotive words to influence the reader

The words we select to describe something influence how the reader or listener understands the subject. Language can be broadly split into three different emotive categories, as shown below:

Negative feelings	Neutral (no) feelings	Positive feelings
mud brown	mid-brown	golden brown

Task 8 Categorising

Rearrange the following words and phrases so that each group of three begins with the negative term, followed by the neutral term and then the positive term.

small child   cute toddler   little brat

cosy room   poky room   small room

slim   skinny   thin

uncontrollable   lively   occasionally disruptive

Task 9 Using emotive language

Below are three fairly neutral phrases describing aspects of communication. Replace the emboldened words with a negative term and a positive one.

Negative feelings	Neutral (no) feelings	Positive feelings
the invasive Internet	the **fast-growing** Internet	the welcome spread of the Internet
	the chatroom **phenomenon**	
	the **latest** computers	

You may want to use some of the words below, or a dictionary or thesaurus for help.

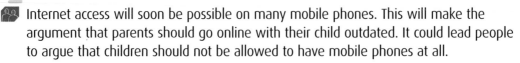

time bomb   state-of-the-art   opportunity   new-fangled

Task 10 Writing

Internet access will soon be possible on many mobile phones. This will make the argument that parents should go online with their child outdated. It could lead people to argue that children should not be allowed to have mobile phones at all.

Discuss the best single argument for why children should be allowed to have mobile phones. Draft a paragraph for a letter to a newspaper putting this point. Remember to:

- make your point, back it up with evidence and drive it home
- use emotive language to persuade your reader
- anticipate the audience's main objection and argue against it.

Getting the structure right

AIMS

- Analyse and compare the overall structure of opinion letters.

- Explore the different ways the paragraphs have been linked.

- Explore and compare different methods of grouping sentences into well-focused paragraphs.

- Develop and signpost arguments in ways that make the logic clear to the reader.

In this section you will consider how to make argument text coherent and cohesive.

Linking sentences and paragraphs effectively

To write an effective argument you need to decide on the points you want to make and order them logically. Then make sure that each paragraph develops its points cohesively and is linked to the following paragraph. The annotations for letter 1 on page 98 show how this writer has ordered and connected her argument effectively. The annotated text skeleton for letter 3 below shows that the points within the paragraphs are linked well but that the links between the paragraphs are not clear enough. (For an explanation of cohesion, see page 87.)

3. Virtually on the Streets

Conclusion

Points flow logically, outlining problem and building up to solution.

Links between paragraphs generally not brought out, though final paragraph echoes theme of opening paragraph.

A. Some parents used TV as babysitter
- Kids exposed to violence – made them violent
- Internet now being used as babysitter

B. Parents should be vigilant when children on Net
- Turn it off

C. Wouldn't allow children to use Net by themselves
- Free access to web like hanging around streets late at night → Powerful image but not linked to opening point of paragraph
- Same dangers

D. Parents should have more time for children
- Play more active role in upbringing → 'If the child wants to' links the practical solution to key point being made
- Go on line with them → 'the same amount of time' links back to opening point about TV

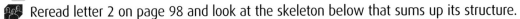
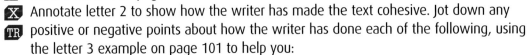

Task 11 — Analysing cohesion

 Reread letter 2 on page 98 and look at the skeleton below that sums up its structure.

☒ Annotate letter 2 to show how the writer has made the text cohesive. Jot down any

TR positive or negative points about how the writer has done each of the following, using the letter 3 example on page 101 to help you:

- How successful has the writer been in ordering his or her points logically?
- How well has he signposted his letter so that the reader sees how one paragraph follows on logically from the next?
- How well does each paragraph link and develop the points within it?

Be prepared to present your ideas.

2. Program Safety

A. Internet not dangerous ✳
- Millions access it daily
- We only get to hear of hackers and paedophiles

B. Programmes like MSN Messenger mean only talk to people who know your address ✳
- Parents should encourage children to use these programmes
- and use less secure software safely

C. Children will be attracted to what is forbidden ✳

Task 12 — Planning practice

 Below are four arguments for why the Internet could be seen as dangerous.

☒ List them in order of significance, then decide how you would back up each point.

TR Decide how you could join these points and jot down the connecting phrases on the skeleton.

No checks on content of Internet sites, so much of the information may be wrong

Provides paedophiles with an easy way to contact young people

Internet is dangerous

Creates an even bigger gap between the rich and poor in the world

Hackers are determined to create viruses to undermine the system – they might succeed

Sentence structure and punctuation

Making the sentences work

AIMS

Combine clauses into clearly expressed complex sentences, using the comma effectively as a boundary signpost.

Explore the impact of a variety of sentence structures.

Revisiting complex sentences

Look at the different types of sentences below. In total, there are:

- four complex sentences
- three simple sentences
- one compound sentence
- one minor sentence.

Task 13 | Analysing

 Use the grammar panel on page 104 to help you identify what type of sentence each sentences below is.

Then look carefully at how the sentences have been punctuated. Explain why there are:

- no commas in sentence 3,
- one comma in sentence 4,
- two commas in sentence 5,
- three commas in sentence 6.

Be prepared to present your conclusions.

1. <u>The teacher entered the room</u>. <u>The girl quickly closed down the web page</u>.
2. <u>The teacher entered the room</u> and <u>the girl quickly closed down the web page</u>.
3. <u>The girl quickly closed down the web page</u> because the teacher entered the room.
4. Because the teacher entered the room, <u>the girl quickly closed down the web page</u>.
5. The girl, who had seen the teacher enter the room, <u>quickly closed down the web page</u>.
6. Seeing the teacher, whom she'd always disliked, enter the room, <u>the girl quickly closed down the web page</u> because she didn't want him to see what she had been doing.
7. Teacher! <u>The girl quickly closed down the web page</u>.

3 Planning the structure

Now list the key points you would want to argue for in your letter and any potential counter-arguments that you need to anticipate.

Next, decide which point you will make first and how you are going to support it. Order the rest of your points so that the whole letter holds together and builds up to its conclusion.

Use a persuasion text skeleton to help plan your key points and the statements that develop them.

Key points **Supporting points** **Countering statements**

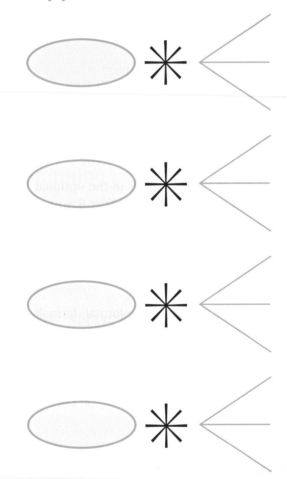

4 Discussing what you are going to write

Take it in turns to present your key points to your partner, trying to develop and link your points as coherently as possible. When you are not presenting, listen carefully and be prepared to offer advice on how to make the argument more coherent. Remember, don't try to influence your partner's viewpoint. Your role is to help them express their view as clearly as possible, not to influence it.

Adapt your plan, if appropriate, in the light of this discussion.

Composing your piece

 Now you are in a position to begin composing your letter.

Points to remember

As you write, remember to:

- begin with a hook that will grab the reader's interest
- make certain that each key point is developed effectively with supporting material within each paragraph (see page 101)
- anticipate responses and objections (see page 99)
- use effective sentence signposts to help your reader follow the argument (see page 99)

- use a range of rhetorical devices – including powerful sentence starters (see page 100)
- vary the structure of your sentences. remember to use short precise sentences as well as more complex ones (see pages 103–104)
- select emotive words that help support your viewpoint (see page 100)
- punctuate sentences correctly.

You may want to use some of the sentence signposts and connectives below.

Sentence signposts and connectives

- Everyone recognises
- We cannot just pretend that
- Technology is advancing more quickly than
- Demand that all Internet providers close down chatrooms

- Moreover
- Furthermore
- Therefore
- Because
- However

 ## Peer comment

 Swap your draft with your partner's and read each other's carefully. Discuss together what works well and highlight this on the draft. Refer back to the reminders above to help you do this.

Now discuss what could be done to improve the quality of the letter and jot down suggestions on the draft.

Redraft the letter using the comments to guide you.

Pulling it all together

 Listen to some of the letters written by members of your class.

 Decide what are the key features that make these letters effective. Be prepared

to feed your ideas back to the class.

Set up to three targets for yourself for improving your ability to present a written argument coherently.

H The Art of Advice Writing

1 How advice text works

AIMS

Explore the key ingredients of advice text.

Make notes on advice text suiting its purpose.

In this section you will learn more about texts that give advice, thinking about their audience, purpose and form, and focusing on their typical structure and language features.

Audience, purpose, form

Texts that give advice come in many forms. Books, leaflets and magazine articles provide advice on everything, from keeping fit to romance to bike maintenance.

When you give advice, you are often combining aspects of several text types:

- **Persuasion**, encouraging the reader to act in a particular way
- **Argument**, giving reasons why the advice is good
- **Information**, providing facts which support the advice
- **Instruction**, advising the reader about how to do something.

However, the features of a persuasion text are normally the dominant ones (see page 78).

TYPICAL FEATURES

The typical features of advice texts are listed below. You will need to refer to these in Section 2.

- The **audience** is someone who needs advice on a topic.
- The **purpose** is to give advice and persuade the reader to take it.
- The form or structure often includes a series of points in a logical order that is clearly signposted, e.g. 'The most important thing to remember is'; presentational devices to make the structure clear, e.g. subheadings, text highlighting and bullet points; an opening to hook the reader, e.g. 'Want to avoid looking like a couch potato?'

Typical **language features** are:

- direct address to the reader, using the second person to provide impact, e.g. 'Have you thought of...'
- a conversational informal tone, making it sound as if you are on the side of the reader. This often includes a 'softened' form of the imperative/command, e.g. 'Go on, try it!'
- clear reasons for why your advice should be followed, often using causal connectives, e.g. 'If you do this...then'

The whole purpose of campaigning is to win support for a particular cause, for example local issues like stopping a school closure, or international issues like global warming.

Read the extract below from the *DIY Guide to Public Relations* by Moi Ali, which offers advice to organisations about how to campaign effectively. One example of each of the language features listed on page 108 has been highlighted. Annotate at least one other example of each feature in the last three paragraphs.

Campaigning

Make sure that you are not, and never become, guilty of the seven deadly sins of campaigning:

Colourful hook – engages the reader's interest

Seven routes to a quick downfall

1. **Being vague[1] about what you are trying to achieve.** Always be absolutely clear about your aims and objectives. Write them down so that everyone has the same understanding of what you are working towards.

Series of points in logical order – numbered to strengthen sequence

Throughout, addresses the reader directly as 'you'

2. **Launching a campaign that is unnecessary.** If another organisation is successfully campaigning on the same issue, join forces, don't compete or duplicate.[2] If there is another way of achieving what you want, do that instead.

Emboldened text – emphasises topic of each point

3. **Talking tommyrot.**[3] Feeling strongly about an issue is important but it's not enough. You need to do research and know what you are talking about. Gather together facts and figures to support your case.

Softened form of imperative – suggests necessity rather than instructing

Conversational tone – reassures the reader

4. **Whatever you do, do it well.** Good presentation need not cost money and it will certainly help you to be taken seriously by others. So adopt a professional attitude at all times.

Clear reasons why advice should be followed

5. **Losing a sense of perspective or becoming fanatical.** However passionately you feel about the issue, try to speak in measured[4] tones and keep your objectivity.[5] That way people will be more inclined to listen and to take notice.

6. **Engaging in internal power struggles and in-fighting.** Remember that you are all on the same side, so don't let your campaign fall apart through in-fighting.[6] Keep your fire power[7] for the real enemy, or you'll end up shooting yourself in the foot.[8]

7. **Letting the morale of your supporters flag.** Whenever you achieve something, however small, let everyone know. It helps maintain[9] interest and gives the impression that the campaign is going somewhere.

[1] **vague** – uncertain

[2] **duplicate** – repeat

[3] **tommyrot** – old-fashioned term for 'rubbish'

[4] **measured** – calm, balanced

[5] **objectivity** – if you are objective, you are not influenced by personal feelings

[6] **in-fighting** – quarrelling between members of the same company

[7] **fire power** – war image meaning arguments

[8] **shooting yourself in the foot** – war image meaning you'll injure yourself and not the opposition

[9] **maintain** – keep

The Art of Writing Advice

Paragraph topics

Advice text often uses topic headings rather than topic sentences to guide the reader through the key points. In this text the writer has seven points to make, signalled by the emboldened text beginning each point.

Task 2 Analysing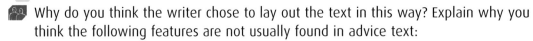

Why do you think the writer chose to lay out the text in this way? Explain why you think the following features are not usually found in advice text:

- figurative language (powerful comparisons that help the reader picture exactly what is being described)
- paragraphs organised in chronological order.

You may want to look back at the typical features on page 108 to help you. Be prepared to present your explanation.

Using text skeletons

In order to understand the structure of a text, it can help to draw a diagram or 'text skeleton'. Text skeletons represent the bare bones of a text.

The shape of an advice text is usually very similar to that of a persuade text because it is made up of a series of points. Therefore, the persuade skeleton (see page 80) can also be used for advice text. In the *DIY Guide to Public Relations*, the bold text identifies the key point, the next sentence expands on the point and the final sentence backs it up (as shown below).

Using text skeletons will help you to analyse the structure of a text, and plan your own writing.

Task 3 Structuring

Below is the beginning of a text skeleton for the extract. Complete the skeleton so that you have a full set of notes on all seven key points of the advice extract.

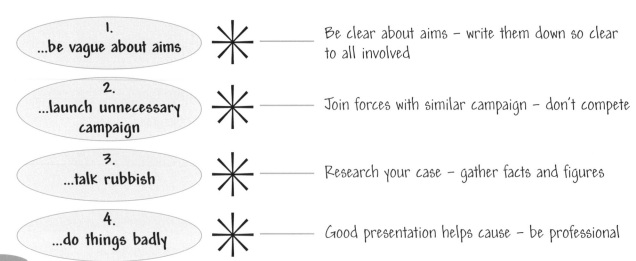

Seven sins of campaigning: never...

1. ...be vague about aims — Be clear about aims – write them down so clear to all involved

2. ...launch unnecessary campaign — Join forces with similar campaign – don't compete

3. ...talk rubbish — Research your case – gather facts and figures

4. ...do things badly — Good presentation helps cause – be professional

Composition and effect

Learning from example

AIMS

Analyse how writers:
- adapt the stylistic conventions of persuasion text to fit writing advice text.
- use a conversational informal tone to sound as if they are on the side of the reader and recognise how this influences word choice.

In this section you will think about the audience and purpose of advice text, and how to compose writing that engages the audience.

Test watch As well as building up your writing skills, the following sections are good preparation for the optional reading tests at the end of Year 8 because they help you:

- comment on a writer's purpose and the effects of the text on the reader
- comment on the structure and organisation of texts
- comment on writers' use of language
- deduce, infer or interpret information, events or ideas
- describe, select or retrieve information, events or ideas from texts.

If you show these skills in the reading test, you will gain a better mark.

Remembering audience and purpose

Usually advice text is aimed at people who are looking for advice on a particular topic. Engaging the reader and then keeping their interest relies on four elements:

- Thinking carefully about the target audience, e.g. children, teenagers, professionals, etc.
- Using a 'hook' that will grab the target audience's attention at the start of your text, e.g. 'the seven deadly sins of campaigning'.
- Selecting the right level of formality to engage the target audience, e.g. 'Wanna be cool?' might be fine for teenagers but would not suit older professionals.
- Selecting the right tone for your audience so that your advice hits home but doesn't sound too bossy, e.g. 'It's often a good idea to drink more water' rather than 'Drink more water'.

Hooking your audience

Newspaper headlines hook the audience and sum up the focus of the article. Headings in advice text serve the same purposes. Below are five alternative headings for the advice text.

Seven things to avoid when campaigning

The seven deadly sins of campaigning

Seven things not to do when campaigning

Seven ways to ensure your campaign fails

Don't do these things if you want your campaign to succeed

Task 4 Discussing

 Decide which headlines are effective and which are not. Then select the most effective, giving reasons to support your choice.

Selecting the right level of formality

The writers of advice texts usually choose a fairly informal tone to try to engage their reader, but this will vary depending on the audience and purpose.

 Task 5 Discussing

 The formal but friendly tone of an advice text can be varied depending on the audience. Below are three different audiences for an advice text, three different levels of formality and three examples. Match the audience and purpose to the appropriate level of formality and example.

Audience 1: Teenage girls worried about spots	Formal and impersonal	Hey there, worried that gorgeous hunk won't even glance in your direction?
Audience 2: Middle-aged women worried about wrinkles	Formal but friendly	Advise patients that a healthy diet helps create healthy skin.
Audience 3: Professionals who advise people on skin conditions	Informal and chatty	Taking care of your skin can help keep it smooth and radiant.

Now write your own advice sentence for teenage boys worried about spots and for adults worried about skin cancer.

Selecting the right tone

There are two tones that can be adopted when writing advice text.

1. Telling people directly what to do or not do, e.g. 'Eat five portions of fruit or vegetables every day and avoid sugary drinks.'

2. Gently suggesting what they might do, e.g. 'It's a good idea to try to eat five portions of fruit or vegetables every day and do your best to resist sugary drinks.'

Task 6 Discussing

 Look back at the advice text on page 109. Which of these tones has the writer chosen? Is it effective? Is one more appropriate for a particular audience than others? Be prepared to feedback your conclusions.

You may want to begin your answers like this:

The direct approach is more suitable for...because...

The more gentle approach is better suited to...because...

Task 7 Writing

 Your task is to write the opening (heading and short paragraph) for an advice text encouraging teenagers in your community not to smoke.

Brainstorm how you might begin such advice. Discuss which idea will make the most effective beginning and which phrase will be best to hook your audience. Consider the tone and level of formality that you will use. Then draft your heading and short opening paragraph, changing it until you think it is just right for your chosen audience.

The Art of Writing Advice

Text structure and organisation

Getting the structure right

AIMS

Adapt the stylistic conventions of persuasion text to fit writing advice text.

Develop and signpost arguments in ways that make the logic clear to the reader.

Look at how writers give advice which takes account of the possible consequences.

Explore methods of grouping sentences into paragraphs of continuous text through logical order and exemplification.

In this section you will think about the best structure for advice text, how to order the points to be made and how to ensure that the paragraphs hang together.

Making the logic clear

The structure and layout of an advice text is very important because it should help convince the reader about the logic of the points being made. Below is the order selected by the writer for the seven deadly sins of campaigning, a sequence that is emphasised by the use of numbers.

1. ...be vague about aims
2. ...launch unnecessary campaign
3. ...talk rubbish
4. ...do things badly

5. ...lose perspective
6. ...engage in in-fighting
7. ...let morale flag

Task 8 **Text skeleton**

 Is this the most logical order for this advice?

TR Which points are definitely in the right place? Could any of the points be moved around to make the piece equally well or even better structured (see right)?

How does the layout help the reader follow the advice? Be prepared to present your conclusions.

For example:

> It might have been better to have swapped points 1 and 2 round so that it began with a more general point about not wasting effort.

Expanding a point

The notes and annotation below sum up how the writer has used three sentences to make a point, expanded it and then backed it up so that the reader is aware of the consequences of the action.

Identifies key point

Seven sins of campaigning: never...

Expands point

1.
...be vague about aims:

Be clear about aims – write down so clear to all involved

Backs up point

Consider points 2 to 7 and see if they could be annotated as on page 113. Has this technique has been maintained for all seven points? Be prepared to provide evidence to support your conclusion.

Using sentence signposts to guide the reader

Identifies key point

Introduces possible scenario that expands key point with a connective

5. Losing a sense of perspective or becoming fanatical. However passionately you feel about the issue, try to speak in measured tones and keep your objectivity. That way people will be more inclined to listen and to take notice.

Links back to scenario consolidating the point

Task 10 **Signposting text clearly**

Analyse point 6 from the campaigning text on page 109 to show how the paragraph has been constructed to make the text hang together, annotating it as point 5 above. Focus on the use of linking phrases or connectives. Be prepared to present your ideas.

Task 11 **Planning practice**

Imagine that you have been asked to write an advice text encouraging teenagers not to smoke. Think of how you might persuade teenagers not to start. Use the brainstorm below to help you, adding any ideas of your own:

Decide on six key points you want to include and then list them in the most effective order. Then, next to each point, show how you would expand the point and back it up. Add any linking phrases or connectives that you would use for each point.

Making the sentences work

AIMS

- Recognise and exploit the use of conditionals and modal verbs when suggesting possibilities.

- Adapt the stylistic conventions of persuasion text to fit writing advice text including how to write lists coherently.

- Explore the impact of using a colon to introduce a list of points.

In this section you will think about how to introduce and express a series of points effectively, as well as how to suggest ideas rather than issue instructions.

Listing points effectively

Advice texts very often include lists of points – just as persuasion and instruction texts do. A neat way to introduce a list is to make an introductory statement followed by a colon, e.g. the first line of 'Make sure that you are not, and never become, guilty of the seven deadly sins of campaigning:' For more help on using colons, see the grammar panel on page 31.

Whether the list is indicated by bullet points, numbers or just a series of points in order, each point should follow on grammatically from the opening statement. The advice text on campaigning on page 109 does this for every paragraph except for one.

Task 12 **Analysing**

Identify the paragraph that does not follow on grammatically and logically from the introductory statement on page 109. What is wrong with the beginning of this paragraph? Discuss what difference this makes to the way the text hangs together.

Making suggestions

Advice texts often rely on gentle language that makes suggestions rather than issues instructions. It aims to persuade rather than instruct. Modal verbs like 'may' and expressions like 'if' help the writer to signal that what follows is a suggestion and not a command (see also page 129).

see the grammar panel on page 31 / page 109 / see also page 129

GRAMMAR

Modal verbs help the writer modify the meaning of verbs. They range from possibility (you *may* prefer to walk) to necessity (you *must* walk).

'Can'/'could', 'may'/'might', 'shall'/'should', 'ought', 'must', 'need' and 'dare' are all modal verbs.

Conditional connectives can also be used to modify meaning because they set the conditions, e.g. *If* it rains, we won't go.

'Although', 'if', 'when', 'in case', and 'as long as' are all conditional connectives.

The Art of Writing Advice

Listing coherently ━━━━━━━━━

Look back at the spider brainstorm on smoking on page 114. Complete the list of all six points following on from the statement below.

> **Six good reasons not to smoke**
> Whenever you feel tempted to smoke,
> remember:
> 1. you can always smell a smoker.
> 2. you will get wrinkles

Read through your completed list and make certain it flows.

Top tip The first bulleted item in the list begins 'you can'. Begin all the following points with a similar grammatical structure, e.g. 'you can', 'you may', 'you will'.

Task 14 **Writing** ━━━━━━━━━

Look at your list of 'Six good reasons not to smoke'. Write the final two paragraphs (points 5 and 6) presenting your closing points. Use the ideas you developed in Task 11 to help you. Remember to make the point, then introduce a possible scenario that illustrates the key point. Make sure that your paragraph flows grammatically from your introductory statement. Check that you have punctuated your paragraph appropriately so that the meaning is clear.

> **Six good reasons not to smoke**
> Whenever you feel tempted to smoke
> remember:
> 5.

5 Composing your own advice

AIMS

- Write advice which offers alternatives and takes account of the possible consequences.

- Develop and signpost advice so the reader can follow it easily.

- Use the appropriate level of formality given your audience.

- Reread your work to anticipate the effect on the reader and revise the style and structure.

Your task

Write clear advice for a magazine article aimed at adult or teenage mobile phone users on how to minimise the annoyance and disturbance of others while texting or speaking.

Test watch This writing task is good preparation for the type of writing required in your English tests because it helps you learn how to:

plan your work so that it is organised logically into well constructed paragraphs that are coherently linked together

compose your writing effectively to match its audience and purpose

selecting appropriate vocabulary

structure your sentences appropriately and punctuate them correctly.

If you show these skills in the optional English test at the end of Year 8, you will gain a better mark.

1 Audience and purpose

Discuss what effect audience and purpose will have on the style of this advice. In particular consider these questions:

Should the style be informal and

friendly, formal but personal or very formal?

How will you persuade the reader to listen to the advice?

2 Brainstorming the content

Every form of communication has its negative, as well as positive, effects. Mobile phones have completely changed communication but they can also be very irritating.

Role play a range of different ways that people use mobile phones in an irritating way. For example, annoying

ringtones or people shouting obvious things like 'I'm on the train'. Be prepared to present your role plays.

Then, on your own, use the scenarios to help you brainstorm all the points about mobile phones that might irritate people.

The Art of Writing Advice

3 Planning the structure

Select an audience for your advice, choosing between teenagers and adults. Given your chosen audience, decide which points from the brainstorm you will deal with and what order will be most effective. Use a persuasion skeleton, like the one below, to help you plan your advice. Decide how you will word the advice on each point, jotting down any useful memory joggers on your skeleton as in the example.

Cool rules for mobiles

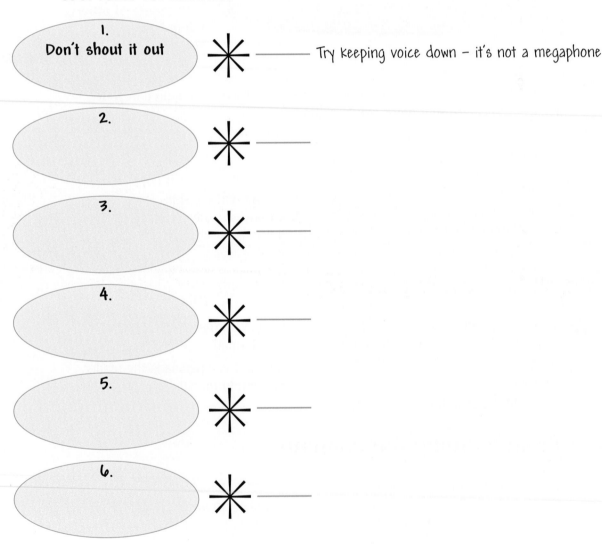

1.
Don't shout it out
*** ———— Try keeping voice down – it's not a megaphone

2.

3.

4.

5.

6.

4 Discussing what you are going to write

Practise talking through your advice with a partner until you think you can express each point clearly. Listen carefully and be prepared to offer help on how to make your partner's advice text more coherent. Adapt your plan in the light of this discussion.

Composing your piece

 Now you are ready to write.

Points to remember

As you write, remember to:

- begin with a hook that will grab the interest of your target audience (see page 111)
- make certain all the points you make flow logically and grammatically from your introductory statement (see page 113)
- lay out your advice effectively (see page 115)
- select the right level of formality and the right tone to suit your audience (see page 112)
- develop each key point effectively, expanding and backing up the point (see page 113)
- use logical/modal connectives to help your points hang together (see page 115)
- check that you have used punctuation correctly especially a colon to introduce your ideas (see page 115).

You may want to use some of the sentence signposts and connectives below to help you.

Sentence signposts and connectives

- Try turning the volume down so you
- You may think your conversation is fascinating but
- Don't spend all your time fiddling with your phone
- Turn your phone off when
- Try setting your phone on vibrate
- Try remembering these points when you
- Ever thought of not shouting

 ## Peer comment

 Swap your draft with a partner's and read it carefully. Discuss together what works well and highlight this on the draft. Use the feedback to write up a final version of your advice text. Include some design features to make the advice attractive and its structure clear to the reader.

Redraft the selected sections of your text, using your partner's comments to guide you.

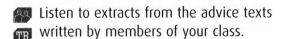 ## Pulling it all together

Listen to extracts from the advice texts written by members of your class.

Decide what are the key features that make these extracts effective. Be prepared to feed your ideas back to the class.

Set up to three targets for yourself for improving your next piece of information writing.

I The Art of Discursive Writing

How discursive text works

AIMS

- Revisit the key ingredients of discursive text.
- Use text skeletons to help analyse and structure discursive text.

In this section you will build on your knowledge of how a discursive text works, thinking about its audience, purpose and form, and focusing on its typical structure and language features.

Audience, purpose, form

Discursive (or discussion) writing is used when you want to analyse an issue from different points of view. Some typical examples are:

- **broadsheet newspaper articles** covering controversial issues, e.g. whether drugs should be legalised

- **student essays** in subjects such as English and History analysis questions, e.g. 'Discuss the causes of the First World War'.

Discursive texts analyse a range of viewpoints or possible causes for something, rather than just seeking to present one viewpoint (argument) or explain something (explanation).

TYPICAL FEATURES

The typical features of a discursive text are listed below. You will need to refer to these in Section 2.

- The **audience** is someone who wants to analyse an issue.
- The **purpose** is to help someone understand an issue by presenting the arguments on all sides as fairly as possible.
- The **form** or structure often includes an opening statement introducing the issue; a series of paragraphs, each presenting at least two views on each point, in a logical order, and supported by evidence and comment; logical connectives, e.g. 'As a result', 'however'; a conclusion summing up the argument rationally – often used to state own viewpoint or suggest a way forward.

Typical **language features** are:

- present tense to make general points, e.g. 'The majority viewpoint is', although evidence will often be in past tense if it refers to things that have happened
- formal and impersonal language using the third person, often including the passive, e.g. 'It could be argued that'
- tentative[1] language – expressing possibility, e.g. 'it could be', 'perhaps', 'if'
- rational, restrained tone and language to present each viewpoint fairly.

[1] **tentative** – hesitant, uncertain

Reading and annotating

  The discursive article below questions the way electronic communication not only transforms how we can find out information, but also how much information is known about us. The first half of the article has been annotated to illustrate all the ingredients of a discursive text (see page 120).

Annotate the second half of the text to show another example of as many of these features as possible.

Should We Worry About Google?

Present tense

Series of paragraphs – present a range of viewpoints

Logical connective – signals change of direction

Formal, impersonal language

Introduction to the issue

Tentative language – 'should' raises questions

Topic sentence – introducing focus of paragraph

Sentence signposts – add information. Note restrained tone

Evidence – backs up point

Every day, Google processes over 200 million web search requests, taking a fifth of a second to scan an index of 3 billion web pages. But should people be worried about asking Google?

Everyone who uses the net loves Google because, if you want information quickly, you see Google as a friend. But if you use Google, it knows a lot about what you are worried about, as well as where you shop and what you're interested in. What many Googlers are not aware of is that each time you search Google, it records what you searched for. Daniel Brant, the creator of Google-watch.org, expresses it as 'a window into your state of mind'.

However, Google says that although it intends to keep its records for 35 years, it has no plans to sell or release them. But will this stop governments getting information? For example, the Patriot Act enables the US government to force Google into sharing its massive database as part of its war against terrorism, if it so chose.

Moreover, Google can be a worry for organisations as well as governments and individuals. For example, the Church of Scientology is furious that the site listed second in a Google search for "scientology" turns out to be Xenu.net, which is run by a fierce opponent of the cult.[1] Last year the Church's lawyers successfully bullied Google into removing links to Xenu.net and similar sites, until a public outcry forced a climb-down.

It could be argued that Google is a threat to individual freedom. But knowing that probably won't make any difference; most of us will carry on using it because it's so good at solving our immediate problems.

5

10

15

20

25

30

[1] **cult** – a certain type of religious worship

The Art of Discursive Writing

Topic sentences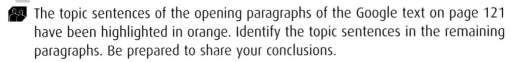

The topic sentences of the opening paragraphs of the Google text on page 121
have been highlighted in orange. Identify the topic sentences in the remaining
paragraphs. Be prepared to share your conclusions.

The topic sentence in the introductory paragraph is not the first sentence in the
paragraph. Why do you think writers sometimes do not place the topic sentence at
the beginning of a paragraph?

Using text skeletons

In order to understand the structure of a text, it can be useful to draw a diagram
or 'text skeleton'. Text skeletons represent the bare bones of a text.

A typical discursive skeleton, like the one below, shows a series of points (the
asterisks) moving down the page in a logical order. Each major point has a
contrasting viewpoint in the opposite column. You could think of the two columns
as the two opposing arguments, or as the points 'For' and 'Against' a particular view.

The main points, e.g. 'Records what is searched for', are generally backed up by examples,
argument or evidence before the opposing point is made. These supporting statements, e.g.
'Window into state of mind', can be added as lines from the main point and are known as memory
joggers.

Using text skeletons will help you to analyse the structure of a text, take notes on the text and
plan your own writing.

Task 3
Structuring

Below is a partially-completed text skeleton for *Should We Worry About Google?*

The letter labels help you see how the two sides of the argument are developed.

Work out how you would complete the final memory joggers for the conclusion.

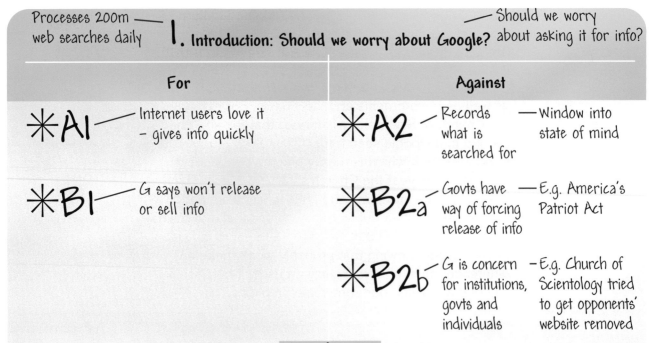

Composition and effect

Learning from example

AIMS

- Consider how the writer has weighed different viewpoints and presented a balanced analysis.
- Appreciate the impact of figurative language in text.
- Recognise bias and objectivity distinguishing fact from theory or opinion.
- Consider how the writer has integrated evidence to support the analysis.

In this section you will read an essay on the significance of television in children's lives and comment on the style in which the debate has been presented.

Test watch As well as building up your writing skills, the following sections are good preparation for the optional reading tests at the end of Year 8 because they help you to:

- comment on a writer's purpose and the effects of the text on the reader
- comment on the structure and organisation of texts
- comment on writers' use of language
- deduce, infer or interpret information, events or ideas
- describe, select or retrieve information, events or ideas from texts.

If you show these skills in the reading test, you will gain a better mark.

Task 4 · Topic sentences

 Below is a short discursive essay considering the effect of television on children. The best way of understanding what a text is saying is to look for the topic sentences, the first two of which have been highlighted in orange.

As you read, identify the topic sentences in the remaining six paragraphs. Check with a partner that you agree on what these topic sentences are.

Is Television Helping or Harming our Children?

Ever since television started to become **part of the furniture** of the home in the 1950s, debate has circled around the issue of whether or not it harms children. Many parents feel very grateful to television because it helps keep the children occupied but others are worried that it might be damaging their children's mental and/or physical development.

Causal connective – explains a viewpoint

Tentative language – 'might' raises questions

Topic sentence – introduces overall topic

Formal, impersonal language – includes the passive

Present tense

First, it is worth considering how widespread television watching has become. A recent report found that television – increasingly a **box** in every bedroom – is like a "**noisy lightbulb**" that is never switched off. Some children cannot imagine life without it. "The television is **almost like a member of the family in its own right**," the report said. The research, carried out from 1996 to 2001 and published by the broadcasting standards commission and the independent television commission, found that most children kept the TV on while doing their homework. Most parents said they were unwilling to cause trouble by turning it off and gave way easily to pressure: "They're always, like, 'Please, please, please, I have to watch it!'" said a London father.

Parents who support TV watching argue that it helps them by keeping their children occupied and entertained. They defend allowing children to have their own TVs in the bedroom by saying that this means that children can watch specialist programmes without disturbing the rest of the family, and thus youngsters have more access to educational programmes.

Moreover, it could be argued that children who are not allowed to watch television are shut out of conversations with friends about what programmes they have seen. The child who is denied access to TV could thus feel very isolated and might, therefore, perform badly at school. In addition, interestingly, some research suggests the ability to understand stories on the television at the age of six is a good predictor of how well children will understand stories when reading them at the age of eight.

On the other hand, parents who are worried about the dominance of television tend to be concerned not only about programme content but about the mental and physical consequences of endless TV-watching.

They argue that children could watch programmes with violent or sexual themes if they turn on television after the watershed and that unsupervised youngsters could watch excessive amounts of television without parents being aware of it. In addition, they fear that television might be undermining children's creativity since time spent watching TV could be spent on imaginative play. Thus children might fail to learn how to entertain themselves through games and creative play which are an important foundation for learning. Related to this concern is the fear that excessive TV-watching may mean children fail to learn social skills because they don't interact with other children.

Finally they are concerned that youngsters are liable to become **couch potatoes** and be at risk of becoming overweight as they sit in front of the television stuffing their faces with crisps and chocolate.

Whatever is the truth about the effects of television, one thing is clear from the survey results: television is here to stay. Rather than opposing television, which would be unrealistic, it is

Sentence signpost – introduces new paragraph. Note restrained tone and use of third person

Series of paragraphs – presents a range of viewpoints

Past tense – signalling events that have happened

Evidence – backs up point

10

15

20

25

30

35

40

45

50

perhaps worthwhile to consider whether any limits should be 55
recommended for very young children's exposure to television.
For example, should there be a recommended age limit below
which parents would be discouraged from allowing children to
have their own television set in their bedrooms? Are we so sure
that television is a good thing that we would encourage every 60
child to have its own television from the earliest possible age?

Task 5 **Annotating**

Annotate the next two paragraphs of the text to show another example of as many
of the typical features of discursive text as possible (see panel on page 120).

Writing an effective introduction

Key tasks for anyone writing a discursive essay are to:

- introduce the topic in a way that interests the reader
- not distort the various viewpoints that are being analysed.

Task 6 **Analysing**

Reread the opening paragraph of the essay on page 123, considering these questions:

- What features can you identify that may help to grab the reader's interest?
- What evidence is there that the writer's introduction is balanced (that is, not
  biased in favour of one particular viewpoint)? For example, 'debate has circled'
  suggests a debate that keeps going round and round with many viewpoints.

Using figurative language

Including images that maintain the reader's interest can be as important in a discursive essay as
in a story. In an essay, they can often add life to generalisations or make a point seem more real.
Some of the figurative language (in bold in the text) appears in the grid below.

Task 7 **Discussing**

Discuss what makes each of the phrases and quotations below effective.

Image	What makes it effective?
part of the furniture	a memorable way of expressing that it has become a part of everyday life
circled	
box	
noisy lightbulb	
almost like a member of the family	
couch potatoes	

What qualities/effects do the quotations in paragraph two add to the essay?

Presenting fact, theory or opinion

It is very important when writing a discursive essay to distinguish between:

- **fact** (an event or thing known to have happened or existed)
- **theory** (a suggestion or set of ideas that is put forward based on evidence)
- **opinion** (judgement or belief not based on certainty or proof).

It is important not to misrepresent information.

Task 8 · Interpreting

Look at this statement:

Martian communication systems are superior to those on Earth.

The writer sounds sure of their facts. In reality, however, it is not known if there is life on Mars, let alone sophisticated communication systems. Each of the signposts A–F could be used to introduce this sentence to show that it is either an interesting theory, or a rather ill-founded opinion or a long-established fact.

Place each of the signposts below under the heading that best fits its purpose.

1. Suggests what follows is an opinion and questions its logic	2. Suggests what follows is a fact	3. Indicates uncertainty (it's only a theory)

A How could anyone argue that

B Research has established that

C It is possible that

D There is now overwhelming evidence that

E Such people even declare that

F No one can be sure that

Looking at the quality of the evidence

Just because there is evidence supporting something, it doesn't make it true. It is the quality of the evidence that will lead us to decide if something is true or not.

Task 9 · Writing

Complete the paragraph begun below that questions the logic of the claim that Martian communication systems are superior to those on Earth. Use the information about Mars in Task 8, plus the fact that recent evidence suggests that there may be water and, therefore, life on Mars.

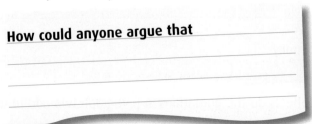

How could anyone argue that

Getting the structure right

AIMS

- Make notes choosing a form that suits the purpose.
- Consider how to structure discursive essays.
- Consider how the writer has grouped sentences into well-focused paragraphs and the different ways paragraphs and ideas have been linked using connectives and sentence signposts.

In this section you will think about different ways of structuring discursive essays and how to link your ideas effectively.

Structuring a discursive essay

There are basically two ways to structure a discursive essay about opposing viewpoints.

Structure A

- Introduce the essay and then go through each point in turn explaining the two opposing positions.
- Conclude your essay drawing out some key points from the debate.

This structure means that you are jumping from one argument to the other as you express the pros and cons of each point. Hence the need for logical connectives to link paragraphs.

Structure A would look like this:

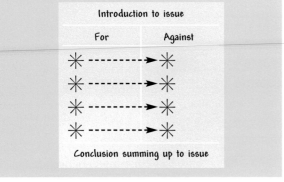

Structure B

- Introduce the issue, then select one viewpoint and go through all the key arguments relating to it.
- Next, present the opposing viewpoint (possibly referring back to the points made on the first viewpoint).
- End with a conclusion drawing out some key points from the debate.

Structure B is summed up by this text skeleton:

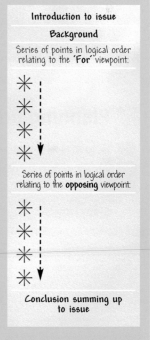

Decide which of the two structures, A or B, the writer of the essay on page 123 has used. Use the skeleton you chose to note the key points made in the essay.

Add memory joggers to flesh it out. As the essay begins with an introduction and then has a paragraph providing some background before presenting the two different viewpoints, remember to add a background section to the skeleton. Be prepared to present your notes.

The Art of Discursive Writing

Signposting the text

Sentence signposts and connectives direct the reader by signalling in what direction the text is moving by highlighting a link. They can indicate:

- **Opposition** – 'in contrast'; 'This is contradicted by'
- **Similarity** – 'equally'
- **Addition** – 'furthermore' 'and'
- **Emphasis** – 'worst of all'; 'This underlines'
- **Complexity** – 'even more confusing'
- **Causal links** – 'as a result'; 'This causes'
- **Temporal** (time-related) **links** – 'from that point on'; 'It was six years later'

Task 11 — Categorising

Below are 13 sentence signposts and connectives from the essay on pages 123–125. Group these under the headings in the grammar panel above. There may be several examples under some headings and just one under others.

Ever since	In addition	Related to this
because	On the other hand	Finally
but others are worried	not only...but also	Whatever is the truth about
First	since	Rather than Moreover

Task 12 — Planning practice

Below is one possible way to structure an essay on the advantages or disadvantages of television for young children. Discuss the sentence signposts in the grammar panel above in order to fill in the blank boxes that introduce or link the points.

Structure A

Introduction to issue

Signposts/ introducing points	For		Signposts/ contrasting points		Against
1.	1. Entertains children and keeps them happy	✱	1.	✱	1. Makes children very passive
2.	2. Helps children learn language because they hear such a range of language	✱	2.	✱	2. Stops children learning language because they just listen and watch and don't speak
3.	3. Helps children understand the world		3.		3. Exposes young children to things they shouldn't know about
Intro conclusion:		✱		✱	

Conclusion summing up issue

Sentence structure and punctuation

Making the sentences work

AIMS

- Use a variety of sentence structures effectively, making good use of the full range of punctuation.

- Recognise and exploit the use of tentative language when speculating, hypothesising or discussing possibilities.

- Construct discursive paragraphs effectively that make a point that is well supported by evidence and comment.

In this section you will think about how to express points indicating uncertainty as well as write effective discursive paragraphs backing up points.

Being tentative

Discursive essays should analyse a range of viewpoints in an unbiased[1] way. Such writing requires a tentative (hesitant) way of expressing ideas so that the writer makes suggestions and explores possibilities, keeping their options open, rather than presenting the issue as straightforward and unproblematic. Modal verbs like 'may' and expressions like 'if' help the writer to signal that what follows is a possibility rather than a fact, as well as tentative phrases and verbs like 'It is possible' and 'suggests'.

[1] **unbiased** – not favouring one side; not prejudiced

GRAMMAR

Modal (or conditional) **verbs** help the writer modify the meaning of verbs. They range from possibility (you *may* prefer to walk) to necessity (you *must* walk).

'Can'/'could', 'may'/'might', 'shall'/'should', 'ought', 'must', 'need' and 'dare' are all modal verbs.

Conditional connectives can also be used to modify meaning because they set the conditions, e.g. *If* it rains, we won't go.

'Although', 'if', 'when', 'in case', and 'as long as' are all conditional connectives.

Task 13 | Identifying the conditions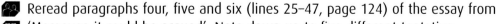

Reread paragraphs four, five and six (lines 25–47, page 124) of the essay from 'Moreover, it could be argued'. Note down up to five different tentative expressions, commenting on what difference the expressions make to the meaning of the text. Be prepared to present your findings.

The conditional challenge

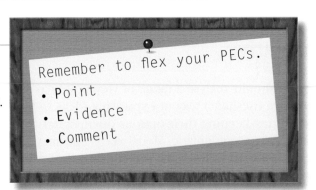

One of you is a student and the other a History teacher. The student is attempting to explain that they may not get their History project completed by the deadline. The teacher is insisting that they must.

Improvise their conversation, ensuring that the student uses tentative language ('I'm not certain if', 'I may not') while the teacher uses expressions that emphasise necessity ('You must', 'It is essential'). Be prepared to present your role play.

When listening to the role plays of others, jot down in two columns all the different expressions that indicate:

Uncertainty	Necessity

Presenting evidence

Discursive writing involves presenting a range of contrasting points clearly, backing each one up with evidence and reinforcing it with a comment.

Remember to flex your PECs.

- Point
- Evidence
- Comment

Consider the example below:

A survey of 1000 13-year-olds reveals that they feel that there should be a recommended age limit for allowing a child to have a television in their bedroom. 62% felt that this age limit should be four. One boy explained: "It's not right is it, leaving a little kid alone with a telly in their bedroom? You just don't know what sort of programmes they might switch on late at night." This raises the question of how such a recommendation should be introduced.

 Task 15 **Analysing point, evidence, comment**

- Annotate the paragraph above to show the main **Point** being made, the **Evidence** given to support it and the **Comment** made to round off the point.

Task 16 **Flexing your PECs**

Use the information below to write a well-constructed and properly-punctuated paragraph that makes a point, backs it up with evidence and finishes the point with a comment.

A The vast majority of students said TV was on all the time – background noise.

B Only 10% said television in shared areas was often turned off in the evenings.

C "Sometimes it really irritates me. You're trying to explain something that's really important and Mum's not listening because she's watching *Neighbours*."

D Suggestion – encourage people to turn the television off when it's just on as background noise.

AIMS

- Record and analyse views using a questionnaire.

- Weigh different viewpoints and present a balanced analysis integrating evidence to support the analysis effectively.

- Decide on the best structure for your essay.

- Group a variety of sentences into well-focused paragraphs that are effectively linked to provide cohesion and coherence.

- Reread your essay anticipating the effect on the reader and revise style, structure and accuracy as necessary.

Your task

Conduct a survey and then write a balanced analysis of the television viewing habits of your class, bringing out the variety or similarity of viewpoint as appropriate.

Test watch This writing task is good preparation for the type of writing required in your English tests because it helps you learn how to:

- plan your work so that it is organised logically into well constructed paragraphs that are coherently linked together

- compose your writing effectively to match its audience and purpose

- selecting appropriate vocabulary

- structure your sentences appropriately and punctuate them correctly.

If you show these skills in the optional English test at the end of Year 8, you will gain a better mark.

⬡ Audience and purpose

The title of your essay is 'How important is television to the lives of your class and do any aspects of TV-watching cause them concern?' The best essay will be used to take the debate forward either with other classes or parents.

Discuss what effect audience and purpose will have on the style of this

piece of discursive writing. In particular consider these questions:

- Should the style be informal, formal but friendly, or formal?

- How will you back up the points you make?

- How will you help the reader follow your analysis?

⬡ Establishing the content

The content of this essay is based on surveying the TV viewing habits of your class.

Fill in the TV questionnaire on page 132 on your TV viewing habits.

TV questionnaire

Boy/Girl   [Do not put your name on your questionnaire]

A. How important is television?

A1) Tick the one phrase below that best sums up your attitude to TV:

- ☐ of no significance
- ☐ pleasant to have on in the background but don't really watch it
- ☐ watch occasionally
- ☐ watch regularly
- ☐ couldn't live without it

A2) How would you describe the importance of TV to you? (Try and make your quotation interesting/colourful – this will help the article writing later on.)

B. Facts about television in your home

B1) How many televisions are there in your home?

    None   1   2   3   4   more

B1) If NONE, explain why overleaf and ignore the rest of this questionnaire.

B2) Do you have a television in your bedroom?   YES/NO

B2i) If YES, from what age did you have a television in your bedroom?

    1–2   3–4   5–6   7–8   9–10   11–12

B3) Is there at least one television in a communal area like the lounge or kitchen?   YES/NO

B3i) If YES, is that television 'always on'?
(i.e. only turned off when everyone is out or in bed)   YES/NO

B4) On average, how many hours per day do you watch television?

    1   2   3   4   5   6   7   8   9   10   more

C. Issues surrounding television viewing

C1) Do you think there is an age limit below which a child should not have TV in their bedroom? Please indicate your view below.

    no limit   2   4   6   8   10   12   higher

Write a sentence or a series of bullet points explaining your decision.

_____

_____

_____

C2) Do you want to raise any other concerns about television and its effects? YES/NO

If YES, explain your concerns/issues briefly overleaf.

Using a blank questionnaire, record the responses of your group so that you can sum them up. List any additional concerns, ticking each time they are mentioned so that you have an order of importance. Decide which of the quotations will be of most use for the article and note these on your summary.

Be prepared to present the findings of your group clearly so that all the findings can be combined.

Analyse the main viewing habits that emerge and any significant minority differences you may wish to draw out.

 # Planning the structure

 Look at the findings from the survey. The essay question lends itself to the standard discursive essay structure below.

Sketch the highlighted sections of the discussion skeleton below and add memory joggers summing up the key

points arising from the questionnaire, identifying the quotes (evidence) you are going to use and indicating the comments you will make on these.

Introduction

For television, i.e. all the points that show TV is central to person's way of life	**Against television** i.e. all the points that show TV is not very important to person's way of life

 A. **How important television is**

 B. **Facts about television in home**
Bring out facts showing TV central
- no of TVs
- in bedroom?
- always on?
- hours watched

 C. **Issues surrounding television viewing**
- Age limit for TV in bedroom?
- Other concerns
Bring out all the positive points

 A. **How relatively unimportant television is**

 B. **Facts about television in home**
Bring out facts showing TV not central
- no of TVs
- in bedroom?
- always on?
- hours watched

C. **Issues surrounding television viewing**
- Age limit for TV in bedroom?
- Other concerns
Bring out all the negative points

Conclusion

Composing your piece

 Now you are ready to begin writing.

Points to remember

As you write, remember to:

- begin with a hook that will grab the reader's interest while ensuring your introduction is balanced (see page 125)

- flex your pecs: develop each key point effectively, supporting it with evidence and driving it home with a comment (see page 130)

- construct your sentences carefully, combining ideas effectively and varying your sentence structure to maximise their effect (see pages 125–126)

- use tentative language to draw conclusions from the survey, indicating clearly if points are fact, theory or opinion (see page 129)

- use sentence signposts and connectives clearly to guide your reader (see page 128).

You may want to use some of the sentence signposts and connectives below to help you.

> **Sentence signposts and connectives**
> - Only a third of pupils commented that
> - The findings of a questionnaire suggest that television plays a significant
> - A large majority of the students said that
> - On the other hand, a significant minority felt
> - The majority of the class were concerned that
> - Everyone expressed concern
> - Perhaps we need to ask ourselves
> - A few pupils felt that
> - Another student
> - Interestingly
> - Others worried that
> - It might be worth considering

Peer comment

 Swap your draft with a partner's and read it carefully. Discuss what really works well using the bullet points above and highlight this on the draft. Then discuss how you could improve particular sections. Jot down your suggestions on the draft.

Redraft the selected sections of your essay, using your partner's comments to guide you.

Pulling it all together

 Exchange essays so everyone has a chance to read all the essays written by the group. Decide which is the best article written by your group and how you will explain the reasons for your selection.

Be prepared to present your ideas.

Note down the key things that you think you need to improve the next time you write a discursive essay.

J The Art of Review Writing

How review text works

AIMS

- Revisit the key ingredients of review writing and its likely impact on readers.

- Analyse the structure of reviews and use this to take notes on its content.

In this section you will deepen your knowledge of how review text works, focusing on its audience, purpose and form and its typical structure and language features.

Audience, purpose, form

There are two main types of review. The first is a self-evaluation of something you have done, such as a drama task. The second is a discussion of someone else's work, such as a film. This type of review informs and entertains, as well a providing a personal evaluation of how good (or bad) it is. You might write such a review in English or Art. This unit focuses on the second type of review.

Because reviews have many different functions, they combine aspects of several text types:

- **Information**, providing basic facts about the play or film
- **Recount**, giving an outline of the plot
- **Discussion**, listing points both for and against the play or film
- **Persuasion**, persuading the reader/viewer to read/see the book, play or film.

TYPICAL FEATURES

The typical features of a review are listed below. Refer to these in Section 2.

- The **audience** is someone who is thinking of reading the book or seeing the film or play or whatever is being reviewed.
- The **purpose** is to evaluate a book/play/film, etc. in an informative way.
- The **form** or structure often includes an opening statement introducing what is being reviewed, e.g. a museum exhibition; a series of paragraphs, moving from key information and summary, to commentary to a final conclusion; often used by the writer to introduce their own viewpoint, e.g. 'So, if you want a fun-packed evening'.

Typical **language features** of reviews are:

- a friendly and informal tone to get on the side of the reader, e.g. 'Don't bother booking for this yawn of a play'
- sentences packed with detail and relying on expanded noun phrases,[1] e.g. 'It was non-stop, side-splitting entertainment from the start'
- the third person to describe the topic, and the first person to give your opinion, e.g. 'This is a great film for all the family and I can't wait to see it again.'
- use of the present tense, e.g. 'The film opens as the police grab'.

[1] **noun phrases** – a noun or a pronoun which can be expanded into a longer phrase, e.g. 'an explosive boat-chase scene' (see page 137)

Task 1 — Evaluating and annotating

The first half of the film review below from *Now* magazine has been annotated to illustrate the features of a review text. Annotate the second half to show another example of as many of these features as possible (see panel on page 135).

Powerful expanded noun phrases – pack in a lot of information

Logical structure – begins with introduction, followed by a plot outline and comment

Friendly, informal tone

Uses key feature of film as hook to interest reader

Wide range of sentence structure – maintains interest

Present tense is the main tense – makes the action seem as if it is happening now

THE ITALIAN JOB

Cert 12A
Released 19 September 2003
Starring Mark Wahlberg, Charlize Theron, Donald Sutherland, Jason Statham

The 1969 original, starring Michael Caine, became something of a cult classic, mainly because of its fabulous chase scenes involving nifty Minis speeding around the city of Rome.

While the cars still remain the stars here, the film makers have sensibly changed the venue.[1] The action starts in Venice with an explosive boat-chase scene followed by an expertly executed gold robbery by mastermind Charlie (Wahlberg), safe cracker John (Sutherland), and their crew (Edward Norton, Seth Green, Jason Stratham and Mos Def). But after being double-crossed by one of his own, Charlie swears revenge.

The action switches to LA, where John's daughter Stella (Theron) comes on board for an even more daring heist.[2] With a fleet of specially modified Minis, the gang decide to steal the gold for a second time – and not even a spot of downtown traffic will stop them.

Although it takes some time to set up the scam,[3] it doesn't interfere with the rhythm of the film and when those Minis hit the highway it becomes a non-stop action flick. Wahlberg, Theron and Norton are solid enough, but it's the comic touches from the support that really stand out – Green as Lyle the techno-nerd, Stratham the getaway man called Handsome Rob and Mos Def, a half-dead explosives expert who's afraid of dogs.

With hardly any swearing, little gratuitous[4] violence and no sex, this is a highly enjoyable romp[5] that the whole family can enjoy. Very va va voom.

NOW rating ★★★★
A surprisingly successful remake of the British heist classic.

[1] **venue** – place the action/event occurs
[2] **heist** – robbery
[3] **scam** – trick or swindle
[4] **gratuitous** – uncalled for, not necessary
[5] **romp** – activity-packed adventure

Topic headings

 Because of the way information is packed into a review, they do not always use topic sentences. Instead, each paragraph has a clear focus. The focus of the first three paragraphs has been written opposite. Add the focus of the final three paragraphs.

List of Key information

1. Intro original film
2. Intro remake
3. Plot development
4. _____
5. _____
6. _____

Structuring reviews

Because reviews are a mixture of different text types, none of the standard text skeletons fits (see page 135). However, a series of headings summing up what is to be focused on, like the one you have just completed, can act as a typical planning frame for reviews.

Task 3 **Structuring**

 Complete the planning frame below for the last two sections so you have a
  complete set of notes on *The Italian Job* review.

Parargraph focus

1.
Intro original film   — 1969 – Michael Caine – cult classic – car chase

2.
Intro remake   ✳ — Still cars – set in Venice – gold robber double-crossed

3.
Plot development   ✳ — Action now in LA – resteal gold

4.
   ✳ —

5. and 6.
   ✳ —

The Art of Review Writing

Learning from example

AIMS

- Consider how a film review takes account of the context for which it was written and its likely impact on readers.

- Explore the effects of using the present tense for vividness.

- Appreciate how formality influences word choice and the impact of informal and figurative language.

In this section you will analyse how a film review has been written to engage the reader's interest.

Test watch As well as building up your writing skills, the following sections are good preparation for the optional reading tests at the end of Year 8 because they help you to:

- comment on a writer's purpose and the effects of the text on the reader
- comment on the structure and organisation of texts
- comment on writers' use of language
- deduce, infer or interpret information, events or ideas
- describe, select or retrieve information, events or ideas from texts.

If you show these skills in the reading test, you will gain a better mark.

Writing an effective introduction

If the introduction to a review fails to grab the reader's attention, they will not read on. Packing in interesting information in an entertaining way is crucial to effective review writing.

Task 4 Analysing

   Look at the three versions of the introduction to the film review below. Decide which is the most effective and which the least. Give reasons why. (Use the Typical Features panel on page 135 to help you.) Be prepared to present your conclusions.

Version 1

The 1969 original, starring Michael Caine, with its fabulous chase scenes involving nifty Minis speeding around the city of Rome, is something of a cult classic.

Version 2

I am going to write a review of *The Italian Job*, a remake of the 1969 version, which starred Michael Caine. I'll tell you about the plot and then what I think of the film as a whole.

Version 3

The first version of *The Italian Job* came out in 1969. It starred Michael Caine. It became famous for its car chase scenes with lots of Minis chasing around the roads of Rome.

Using the present tense for effect

Reviews of plays, books, TV programmes or films are written in the present tense.

Task 5 **Analysing**

Reread the third paragraph on page 136 and compare it with the rewritten version in the present tense below. Decide which one is more effective, and why.

> The action switched to LA, where John's daughter Stella (Theron) came on board for an even more daring heist. With a fleet of specially modified Minis, the gang decided to steal the gold for a second time – and not even a spot of downtown traffic would stop them.

Using informal and colourful language

Reviews are often informal in tone, almost as if the reviewer were chatting to the reader. This is usually combined with figurative language to help the reader to picture the scene.

Task 6 **Analysing**

Shown are versions in more formal English of figurative expressions from the review. Identify the original, more informal, versions and record them, as shown.

More formal and direct alternatives	Original informal version
fast Minis	
city-centre traffic congestion	
reach the main road	
enjoyable action	
very thrilling	
a fast car driver who enables criminals to leave the crime scene swiftly	
a person who is obsessed by technical things	

Now discuss what makes the informal expressions more appropriate and effective for a film review (see page 136 for help). Be prepared to present your ideas.

Task 7 **Describing**

Brainstorm the most exciting car chase or escape scene you can remember from a film or TV, giving details of the elements shown in the spidergram.

How it begins — Near misses — Setting and context — CAR CHASE IN FILM X — How it ends — Appearance of car — Driver

Describe the chase to your partner, making your description colourful and entertaining. Ask your partner to record any colourful expressions you use.

Using the notes made by your partner, and any new ideas you have, draft five colourful expressions that could be used in a review of this scene.

Text structure and organisation

Getting the structure right

AIMS

- Make notes in an appropriate form, which reflect the structure and key content of a review.

- Analyse how the writer has developed ideas within the paragraphs and linked the paragraphs effectively.

In this section you will consider how a text is structured to guide the reader through its meaning, including the overall structure, how the paragraphs connect and how information within paragraphs is linked.

Helping text hang together

If a review is going to hang together effectively, the paragraphs need to link together logically and each paragraph needs to link internally so that the reader can follow what is being said easily. (For more on text cohesion, see page 87.)

The opening of *The Italian Job* review below has been annotated to bring out these links.

Sentence signpost tells reader that plot summary is beginning

Cars provide thematic link between first two paragraphs

> The 1969 original, starring Michael Caine, became something of a cult classic, mainly because of its fabulous chase scenes involving nifty Minis speeding around the city of Rome.
>
> While the cars still remain the stars here, the film makers have sensibly changed the venue. The action starts in Venice with an explosive boat chase scene followed by an expertly executed gold robbery by mastermind Charlie (Wahlberg), safe cracker John (Sutherland), and their crew (Edward Norton, Seth Green, Jason Stratham and Mos Def). But after being double crossed by one of his own, Charlie swears revenge.

The mention of changed venue, followed by the mention of Venice, helps link the paragraph internally.

Sequence and time connectives (highlighted in mauve) guide the reader through plot developments

Task 8   **Analysing**

Reread the rest of the review on page 136. Decide what links the final three paragraphs to the first two paragraphs, and to each other. Consider thematic links, sentence signposts and connectives.

Then identify what helps hold the text together *within* each of these three paragraphs. Again, consider thematic links, sentence signposts and connectives.

Structuring reviews

A planning frame, like the one below, is probably the most helpful support for structuring a review.

- Introduction
- Plot outline
- Comment (often broken into two paragraphs)
- Concluding comment including recommendation.

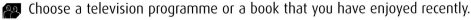

Task 9 **Planning practice**

Choose a television programme or a book that you have enjoyed recently.

Brainstorm the key plot details, character detail or exciting moments. Then work out the planning frame and supporting points. Add the topic sentences that will show the reader the direction the text is going in. For example:

Planning frame   **Supporting points**   **Topic sentences**

Introduction

Plot outline

General comment

Conclusion

Spellbound

* Unbelievable – spellbound by film on spelling and haven't even heard of most of words – spelling bee is big American tradition

* Dramatic documentary of the journey of eight children to finals of American national spelling competition – really get involved with children's feelings. Real insight, e.g. Angela, Mexican immigrant parents – father doesn't speak English – she taught herself spelling, e.g. Harry – hyperactive – endless wit

* Roller coaster of emotions: disbelief, sympathy, understanding, hope, tension, humour, real humanity. At first laugh at them but in end laugh with them and recognize yourself

* Great entertainment for all family

> It's incredible that a film about something as boring as spelling can literally be spellbinding.

> The story introduces you to eight of the contenders in turn.

> The film provides real insight into what motivates people.

> I found myself smiling from the first moment.

Making the sentences work

AIMS

- Analyse the impact of using of a variety of sentence structures including noun phrases and adjectival phrases.

- Punctuate your sentences appropriately with a focus on hyphens.

- Analyse how the writer has combined clauses effectively into complex sentences, using commas appropriately to help the reader follow the meaning.

In this section you will consider how to use expanded noun phrases and adjectival phrases effectively to inject detail into review text.

Injecting interesting detail

Expanded noun phrases can be an excellent way of getting rich detail into sentences.

GRAMMAR

Noun phrases can be a single word (a noun or a pronoun, e.g. 'Dave'/'he'), which can be expanded into a larger phrase. As you can see from the examples below, you can expand noun phrases in a variety of ways, adding words or clauses before or after the original noun or pronoun at the centre of the phrase.

Think about how the noun phrase '*He*' has been expanded in the sentences below.

1. *He* *watched.*

2. *The boy* *watched.*

3. *The fascinated boy* *watched.*

4. *The fascinated boy* *watched* **hoping his hero would evade the claws of the advancing raptors.**

5. Hoping his hero would evade the claws of the advancing raptors, the fascinated boy *watched.*

Beware of overdoing it. This is a sentence but it has become awkward because it is overwritten.

6. *The fascinated boy*, who was hoping his hero would evade the claws of the advancing raptors, *watched.*

Task 10 **Expanding noun phrases** ━━━━━

 Expand the short noun phrase below but leave out the final overwritten example.

- **She** *shouted.*

Be prepared to present your sentences.

Using hyphens

Hyphens join words together for a range of purposes.

1 **Hyphens** are used **to join words together to form compound words**, e.g 'user-friendly'. When a word combination has been used for a long time, the hyphen is often dropped. Sometimes more than one version is used. For example, at a recent Internet exhibition, stands advertised 'on line', 'on-line' and 'online' services.

2 Hyphens are used **to join the syllables of words that are broken at the end of a line of writing** to warn the reader that the word is continuing (see example A).

> **A** When you have finished, it is essen-
> tial that ...

Warning! Remember that words can only be broken up at syllable breaks, rather than at the precise moment you run out of space. Example B is wrong because it breaks the pattern of meaning in the reader's head.

> **B** When you have finished, it is essenti-
> al that ...

3 Hyphens can be used **to give phrases, clauses or sentences an adjectival function**. The adjectival phrase is highlighted in the following examples.

- *The teacher looked at the boy with her <u>don't-even-think-of-doing-that</u> expression on her face.*
- *The <u>never-to-be-forgotten</u> car chase.*

Hyphens are only needed when the adjectival phrase is placed in front of the noun. If it follows the noun, the hyphens are omitted.

- *The teacher looked at the boy with an expression that said don't even think of doing that.*
- *The car chase was never to be forgotten.*

Task 11 **Understanding hyphens**

Match the examples below to the three explanations above of how hyphens are used.

1 100-metre race
2 half-baked ideas
3 pre-war Europe

4 a not-quite-certain-what-to-do-next expression
5 It was completely horri-
fying. I stared in fear

Task 12 **Punctuating adjectival phrases**

Look back at use 3 of the hyphen in the grammar panel above. Then rephrase the following descriptions.

1 The performance was never to be forgotten.
2 The nail was three inches.

3 The girl with blue eyes.

Task 13 **Expanding noun phrases**

 Devise a simple, short explanation for an eight-year-old child on how to use hyphens.

Task 14 **Writing**

Think of a toy that you really loved when you were little. Picture all the features that made you like it and jot down some of the words and phrases that come to mind.

Now turn these phrases into colourful sentences, using expanded noun phrases and adjectival phrases. Contrast these with short, simple sentences.

You may want to adapt this opening to begin your description:

> My teddy wasn't one of those large look-at-me-aren't-I-the-cuddliest-teddy-in-the-world sort of teddy. He was very small, rather hard and a somewhat-dirty shade of brown. But I loved him.

Avoiding confusing commas

In complex sentences that already contain commas, clauses are often separated off by dashes or brackets to avoid confusion. See page 46 to remind you.

Task 15 **Analysing**

 Reread Extract 1 *The Italian Job* review. Analyse the ways in which commas, brackets and hyphens have been used. Be prepared to present your conclusions.

Extract 1

> The action starts in Venice with an explosive boat chase scene followed by an expertly executed gold robbery by mastermind Charlie (Wahlberg), safe cracker John (Sutherland), and their crew (Edward Norton, Seth Green, Jason Stratham and Mos Def).

Decide how you would replace some of the commas with brackets or hyphens in Extract 2 to make the meaning clearer.

Extract 2

> You probably don't know Park and Lloyd by name, but you may know their work: *Wallace & Gromit*, an award-winning series of shorts based on the adventures of a daft inventor and his resourceful dog, or *Creature Comforts*, a truly marvellous, Oscar-winning short featuring interviews with some 'claymation' zoo residents.

AIMS

- Write a critical review of a film, taking into account its context and likely impact on its audience, integrating evidence to support your findings and revise it to suit its audience and purpose.

- Explore the impact of a variety of sentence structures with particular emphasis on effective noun phrases, that are correctly punctuated.

- Develop your ideas within and between paragraphs so that the text is cohesive.

- Explore the effects of using the present tense for immediacy.

Your task

Write a four- or five-paragraph review of a well-known film that would make teenagers or adults want to go and see it.

Test watch This writing task is good preparation for the type of writing required in your English tests because it helps you learn how to:

- plan your work so that it is organised logically into well constructed paragraphs that are coherently linked together

- compose your writing effectively to match its audience and purpose

- selecting appropriate vocabulary

- structure your sentences appropriately and punctuate them correctly.

If you show these skills in the optional English test at the end of Year 8, you will gain a better mark.

1 Audience and purpose

Discuss what effect audience and purpose will have on the style of this review. In particular consider these questions:

- Should the style be informal and friendly, formal or very formal?

- How will you grab the reader's attention?

- How will you pack key information into so few paragraphs?

2 Brainstorming the content

Brainstorm any films that you have seen that have made a lasting impression. Can you agree on any that all or most of you have seen?

Pool your ideas with those of other groups. Establish five that you have enjoyed, with everyone having seen at least one. Select the film that you are

going to review and work with a group which has chosen the same film.

Brainstorm the key plot features, and the characters and stars who played them. Now you will have the basic information from which you can create your review.

Using a planning frame

 Use the review planning frame below to help you structure your review. Against each section, note down the key points that you want to bring out.

- Introduction
- Plot outline
- General comment
- Concluding comment including final recommendation

 ## Composing your piece

Now you are ready to begin writing your review.

Points to remember

As you write, remember to:

- introduce your review in an interesting way (see page 138)
- keep the tone of your review friendly and informal, with some colloquial terms (see page 139)
- use sentence signposts and connectives to guide the reader, and to help the text hang together (see page 140)

- use the present tense for immediacy (see page 139)
- use figurative and colourful language to engage the reader (see page 139)
- use the third person for most of your review but use the first person for your opinion
- engage the reader with interesting and powerful language, including expanded noun phrases and adjectival phrases (see pages 142–144).

You may want to use some of the sentence signposts and connectives below to help you.

> **Sentence signposts and connectives**
> - A blood-curdling adventure for
> - The action starts
> - Set in the year…, this thriller
> - As for the main character
> - The plot gets thickens when
> - …but I felt…
> - If you've never seen a
> - Definitely a film to
> - As the film ended, I…

 ## Peer comment

 Swap your draft with a partner's and read it carefully. Decide together what works really well and highlight this on the draft. Next discuss how to improve particular sections.

Jot down your suggestions on the draft.

Redraft your writing where necessary, using your partner's comments to guide you.

 ## Pulling it all together

 Listen to reviews written by members of your class.

Decide what are the key features that make these extracts effective. Be prepared to feed your ideas back to the class.

Set up to three targets for yourself for improving your next review.

The Art of Review Writing

Exemplars

Key to Colour Coding

Orange	Topic sentences
Mauve	Time connectives
Red	**Connectives of opposition**
Turquoise	Connectives of addition
Pink	**Causal connectives**
Yellow	Simple sentences
Green	Compound sentences
Blue	**Complex sentences**

(A) Narrative exemplars

Task 1 — From line 8

Past tense —

Chronological order — helps the reader understand how one event follows another

> His wife was surprised. 'What are you doing?' she said. 'The baby won't be able to use those things for a long time. Why are you in such a hurry?'
> 'You are quite wrong,' answered her husband. 'Our baby is not an ordinary baby. It came in a week instead of nine months. You see, it will be ready to learn to read and write in a few weeks from now.'
> *Traditional tale*

Third-person narrative – story told by omniscient (all-knowing) narrator

Dialogue – moves the plot on, and gives insight into character

Task 3

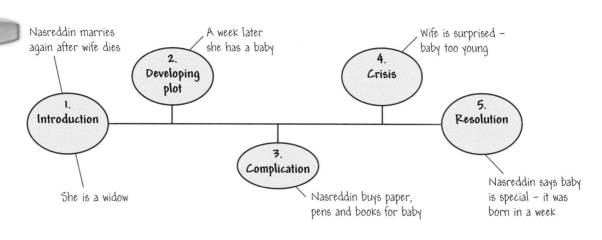

Nasreddin marries again after wife dies

A week later she has a baby

Wife is surprised – baby too young

1. Introduction

2. Developing plot

3. Complication

4. Crisis

5. Resolution

She is a widow

Nasreddin buys paper, pens and books for baby

Nasreddin says baby is special – it was born in a week

Task 6   From line 11:

Expressive and descriptive language – short sentence without a verb strongly suggest the silence

Past tense

Chronological order – helps reader understand how one event follows another

Dialogue – moves plot on. Better than saying 'The examiner then tried a counting exercise'

'What's this?'
Not a sound from Pinpin.
'What's this, then?'
Silence.
'Does he have a hearing problem?'
'No,' said Mrs Hath. 'She can hear you.'
'But he doesn't speak.'
'I suppose there's nothing much she wants to say.'
Bowman and Kestrel held their breath. The Examiner frowned and looked grave, and made a note on his papers. Then he returned to the pictures.
'Well now, Pinto. Show me a doggy. Where's a doggy?'
Pinpin gazed back at him, and neither spoke nor pointed.
'A house, then. Show me a little house.'
Nothing. And so it went on, until at last the Examiner put his pictures away, looking graver still.
'Let's try some counting, shall we, little chap?'
He started counting, meaning Pinpin to follow him, but all she would do was stare. He made another note.

Time connectives – help reader follow chronology of story

Third-person narrative – story told by omniscient narrator

Task 9

1. Tears welled up in her eyes because her birthday was over.
2. He frowned – surely his keys were there a moment ago?
3. Jack still hadn't done his homework. His dad was almost white with fury.
4. Hannah was still lost in sleep when the alarm went off again.

Task 10

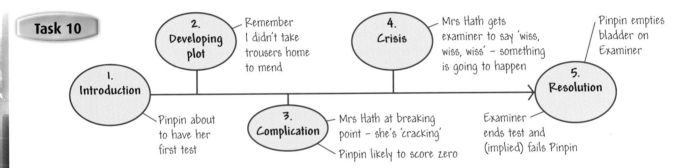

1. Introduction — Pinpin about to have her first test

2. Developing plot — Remember I didn't take trousers home to mend

3. Complication — Mrs Hath at breaking point – she's 'cracking' — Pinpin likely to score zero

4. Crisis — Mrs Hath gets examiner to say 'wiss, wiss, wiss' – something is going to happen

5. Resolution — Pinpin empties bladder on Examiner — Examiner ends test and (implied) fails Pinpin

Task 15

1. Scratching her nose and sniffing, she made no reply.
2. Throwing up his arms in horror he said, 'I don't believe it!'
3. Entering the kitchen, Paula was greeted with a gruesome sight.
4. Overtaking the lorry on a bend, the motorbike skidded into the ditch.

Task 17

On getting to school, Bowman and Kestrel found they had forgotten to bring their homework.
'Forgot?' roared Dr Batch. 'You forgot?'
'Yes, sir.'
'Let's begin at the beginning. Why did you forget?' Dr Batch considered it part of his job to make an example of his pupils.
'Our little sister had her first test this morning,' said Bowman. 'We left the house early, and we just forgot.'
'You just forgot? Well, well, well.' Dr Batch liked lame excuses.

Recount exemplars

Task 1 **From the middle of paragraph 2:**   *Third person*   *Past tense*

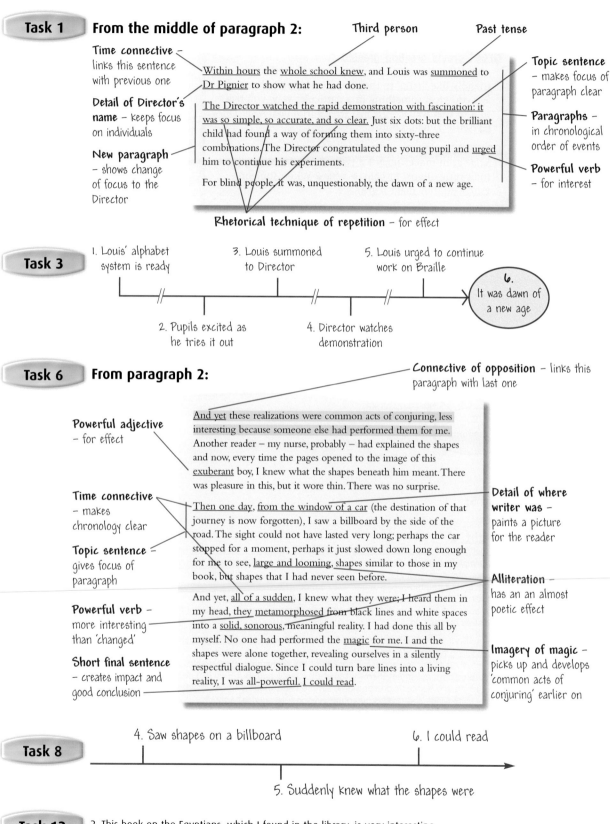

Time connective – links this sentence with previous one

Detail of Director's name – keeps focus on individuals

New paragraph – shows change of focus to the Director

Within hours the whole school knew, and Louis was summoned to Dr Pignier to show what he had done.

The Director watched the rapid demonstration with fascination: it was so simple, so accurate, and so clear. Just six dots: but the brilliant child had found a way of forming them into sixty-three combinations. The Director congratulated the young pupil and urged him to continue his experiments.

For blind people, it was, unquestionably, the dawn of a new age.

Topic sentence – makes focus of paragraph clear

Paragraphs – in chronological order of events

Powerful verb – for interest

Rhetorical technique of repetition – for effect

Task 3

1. Louis' alphabet system is ready
3. Louis summoned to Director
5. Louis urged to continue work on Braille
6. It was dawn of a new age

2. Pupils excited as he tries it out
4. Director watches demonstration

Task 6 **From paragraph 2:**   **Connective of opposition** – links this paragraph with last one

Powerful adjective – for effect

And yet these realizations were common acts of conjuring, less interesting because someone else had performed them for me. Another reader – my nurse, probably – had explained the shapes and now, every time the pages opened to the image of this exuberant boy, I knew what the shapes beneath him meant. There was pleasure in this, but it wore thin. There was no surprise.

Time connective – makes chronology clear

Topic sentence – gives focus of paragraph

Then one day, from the window of a car (the destination of that journey is now forgotten), I saw a billboard by the side of the road. The sight could not have lasted very long; perhaps the car stopped for a moment, perhaps it just slowed down long enough for me to see, large and looming, shapes similar to those in my book, but shapes that I had never seen before.

Powerful verb – more interesting than 'changed'

Short final sentence – creates impact and good conclusion

And yet, all of a sudden, I knew what they were; I heard them in my head, they metamorphosed from black lines and white spaces into a solid, sonorous, meaningful reality. I had done this all by myself. No one had performed the magic for me. I and the shapes were alone together, revealing ourselves in a silently respectful dialogue. Since I could turn bare lines into a living reality, I was all-powerful. I could read.

Detail of where writer was – paints a picture for the reader

Alliteration – has an an almost poetic effect

Imagery of magic – picks up and develops 'common acts of conjuring' earlier on

Task 8

4. Saw shapes on a billboard
6. I could read

5. Suddenly knew what the shapes were

Task 12
2. This book on the Egyptians, which I found in the library, is very interesting.
3. They went on arguing until the neighbours banged on the wall.
4. Feeling hungry, Susan found herself in the kitchen, as usual, and raided the fridge.
5. As the clock struck twelve, there was a knock at the door which woke everyone up.

Exemplars

Task 1 | **From paragraph 2:**

Present tense

Clear heading – shows topic (word entry). The smaller font shows that this is extra detail

Technical terms – relate to subject matter

greet greets greeting greeted

VERB **1** If you greet someone, you say something friendly like 'hello' to them when you meet them. **2** If you greet something in a particular way, you react to it in that way E.G. *He was greeted with deep suspicion.*
▤ (sense 1) hail, salute

Generalised statements

Main meaning given first, less important meaning second

Use of capitals, bold and italic – indicate particular words or syllables, or make it easy to read the text and classification

Icons and abbreviations – replace text and indicate the category of information

grimace grimaces grimacing grimaced
Said "grim-mace" NOUN **1** a twisted facial expression indicating disgust or pain. ▶ VERB **2** When someone grimaces, they make a grimace.

Present tense

Clear headword – shows topic (word entry). The smaller font shows that this is extra detail.

Clear and concise sentences

Formal and impersonal language

Task 3

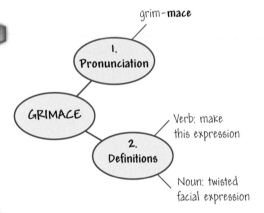

grim-**mace**

1. Pronunciation

GRIMACE

2. Definitions

Verb: make this expression

Noun: twisted facial expression

Task 6 | **Paragraphs 4 and 5:**

Paragraphs – in an order that follows the classification, with subheads to make this clear

Lively use of language – makes a powerful description

Technical terms – relate to subject matter

General statement – followed by example giving detail

Sight 🐾
Visual signals are also used for communication, although they only work at relatively close range. For instance, when a cat arches its back and makes its hair stand on end, she is attempting to frighten you off. Similarly, the black and white stripes of a skunk warn a mountain lion not to approach too close or it will be squirted with its evil-smelling spray. Chimpanzees and apes can even communicate their feelings through facial expressions – just as humans do.

The brilliant colour patterns of many fishes, **reptiles** and birds usually have a signalling function. These visual signals are generally present at all times, such as the red and black colours of the monarch butterfly, which warn predators not to eat them because they taste bad. But they can also be hidden and suddenly presented: when the hawk moth is under attack it unfolds its wings and reveals two huge eyespots to suggest a much bigger and fiercer creature.

Smell 🐈
Chemical signals are widely used by insects, fish and **mammals** as they require little energy to produce. Dogs and cats, among other animals, mark their territory with urine or chemical odours, for example, during the breeding season. Many animals have a sense of smell many times more developed than humans: the scent of the female emperor moth, for example, can attract males more than ten kilometres away.

> **mammal** – an animal that gives birth to live babies and feeds its young with milk, e.g. humans and cats
> **reptile** – a cold-blooded animal with a scaly skin which lays eggs, e.g. snakes and lizards

Topic sentence – introduces key point

Present tense

Clear and concise sentence

Formal and impersonal language

Lively use of language – makes a powerful description

Technical terms – relate to subject matter

Glossary – adds information

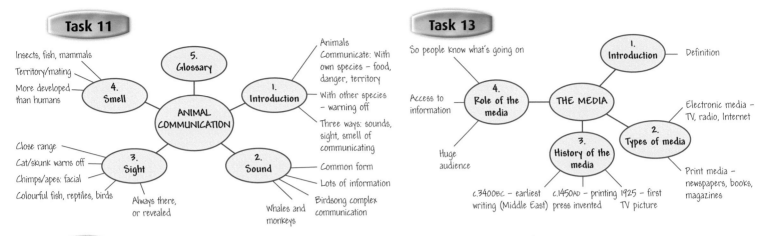

Task 11

Insects, fish, mammals

Territory/mating

More developed than humans

5. Glossary

4. Smell

ANIMAL COMMUNICATION

1. Introduction

Animals Communicate: With own species – food, danger, territory

With other species – warning off

Three ways: sounds, sight, smell of communicating

Common form

Lots of information

Birdsong complex communication

Close range

Cat/skunk warns off

Chimps/apes: facial

Colourful fish, reptiles, birds

3. Sight

Always there, or revealed

2. Sound

Whales and monkeys

Task 13

So people know what's going on

Access to information

Huge audience

4. Role of the media

THE MEDIA

1. Introduction → Definition

3. History of the media

2. Types of media

Electronic media – TV, radio, Internet

Print media – newspapers, books, magazines

c.3400BC – earliest writing (Middle East)

c.1450AD – printing press invented

1925 – first TV picture

D Explanation exemplars

Task 1 — From the end of paragraph 2:

Topic sentence – introduces a step in the explanation

Causal connective – shows link in explanation

Structure – a series of logical steps. The final paragraph goes on to a new point

Causal connective – shows link in explanation

It was, therefore, more and more important to communicate facts – and, above all, to have a record of these facts.

Making a mark on a piece of clay had two great advantages over holding the same information in the brain. First, the writer no longer had to remember what he had written down. And second, the clay became a permanent message, which stayed around whether the messenger was there or not (or even after he had died). Instead of saying, therefore, 'I own two oxen,' the writer could make a mark in a piece of clay which recorded the fact for all to see.

Past tense – because relating events in the past

Formal and impersonal language

Numbering connectives – shows clearly how they link with the 'two advantages'

Task 3

3. Two main advantages of writing

Didn't have to remember   A permanent record for all

Task 6 — From paragraph 3:

Precise technical vocabulary

Simile

Causal language

Present tense

Topic sentence – introduces next step in the explanation

Formal and impersonal language – includes the passive

Metaphor

The vibrations of the eardrum set up further vibrations in a chain of three tiny bones – the hammer, anvil and stirrup. These are arranged in such a way that by the time the vibrations reach the end of the third bone, the stirrup, they have been amplified hugely. They are able to do this rather like a system of levers is able to turn a small movement at one end into a huge and powerful movement at the other.

The sound wave, in the form of the tiny stirrup's powerful vibrations, has now reached the entrance to the inner ear. The inner ear is basically a set of three tubes, together called the cochlea, which wind round each other in a spiral so that they look a bit like a snail's shell. The cochlea is full of fluid, and as the stirrup knocks on what is called the oval window of the cochlea, the fluid within – yes, you've guessed it – vibrates.

The actual organ of hearing, known as the Organ of Corti, lies hidden in the central tube of the cochlea. It contains over 15 000 hair cells. The pressure waves moving through the fluid of the cochlea wash over these highly sensitive cells, and as the hairs waggle and wave like strands of seaweed in the sea, they send electrical signals to the brain along the cochleal nerve.

The signals preserve the correct frequency of the original sound, because different hair cells are affected by different frequencies. They also preserve the correct volume of the sound, because more hair cells are affected when the volume of the sound is higher. So when the brain receives these signals at the end of their lightning fast and exhilarating underground journey, it interprets them as sounds of a precise frequency and volume. It can tell, for example, that the guitar string that was plucked was an A, and that it was plucked very softly.

Causal language

Formal and impersonal language – includes the passive

Topic sentence – introduces next step in the explanation

Causal language

Precise technical vocabulary

Causal language

Structure – series of logical steps. Each paragraph adds another step in the explanation

Causal language

Precise technical vocabulary

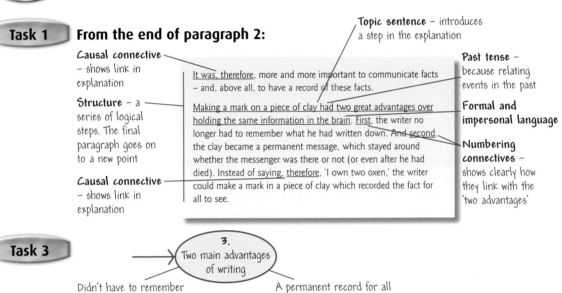

Exemplars

151

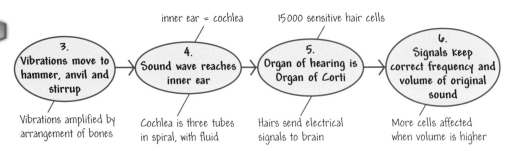

Task 10

3.
Vibrations move to hammer, anvil and stirrup

Vibrations amplified by arrangement of bones

inner ear = cochlea

4.
Sound wave reaches inner ear

Cochlea is three tubes in spiral, with fluid

15000 sensitive hair cells

5.
Organ of hearing is Organ of Corti

Hairs send electrical signals to brain

6.
Signals keep correct frequency and volume of original sound

More cells affected when volume is higher

Task 15

Mailing lists can also be used as a form of online chat between friends; they are, however, not as immediate as chat programs, **as** they don't work in 'real time'. Mailing lists are usually handled by a 'list server', **which** is a special program that automatically sorts the incoming messages, **and** then sends them out to all the current list subscribers. That can be a lot of messages: it is important not to subscribe to too many lists, **as** you may end up with hundreds of messages every day.

(E) Instruction exemplars

Task 1

From instruction 3:

List format – numbers show clear sequence

Imperative – shows it's a command. Each step begins with an imperative, which helps the sequencing.

Use of second person – to address reader

3.   <u>Press</u> and <u>release</u> the <u>Tuning Up</u> or *Tuning Down button* or turn and release the *Tuning control* to change the <u>frequency</u> up or down.

4.   Adjust the *Volume, Bass and Treble controls* to the required settings.

Use of italic – indicates parts of the radio

Technical language

Instructions – simple, clear and brief

Task 2

Press and release tuning up/down button

3.
Change frequency

Turn and release tuning control button

4.
Adjust volume, bass and treble

5.
Switch off

Press on/off button

Task 3

Some possible entries:

First draft	Final version	Why writer altered text
1. Choice of words 'A good example of this is the following'	'For example'	much shorter, and just as clear
'you'll get what looks like complete gobbledegook'	omitted	doesn't need it – complicates text
2. Choice of sentence length/type 'How did I read it?'	'To decipher a secret message'	Doesn't want to use questions
'Well, look at how the letters in the secret message are grouped'	'The letters in the message above are grouped in 4s, which tells you'	More formal and concise
3. Viewpoint of writer ('I can't think of no easy way to remember this, sorry')	not included	writer doesn't want to show ignorance, or even to refer to herself
'I simply reversed the process'	'simply reverse the process'	imperative instead of 1st person more appropriate
4. Organisation/ presentation of material 'Step 2'	Not used	Steps shown clearly by italics/repetition
'You'll see why later.'	Not used	No need to say this – just tells reader later

Exemplars

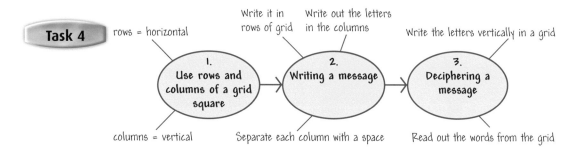

Task 4

rows = horizontal

Write it in rows of grid

Write out the letters in the columns

Write the letters vertically in a grid

1. **Use rows and columns of a grid square** → 2. **Writing a message** → 3. **Deciphering a message**

columns = vertical

Separate each column with a space

Read out the words from the grid

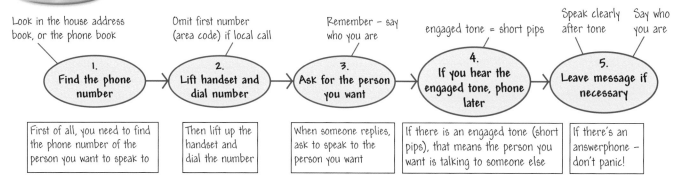

Task 8

Look in the house address book, or the phone book

Omit first number (area code) if local call

Remember – say who you are

engaged tone = short pips

Speak clearly after tone   Say who you are

1. **Find the phone number** → 2. **Lift handset and dial number** → 3. **Ask for the person you want** → 4. **If you hear the engaged tone, phone later** → 5. **Leave message if necessary**

| First of all, you need to find the phone number of the person you want to speak to | Then lift up the handset and dial the number | When someone replies, ask to speak to the person you want | If there is an engaged tone (short pips), that means the person you want is talking to someone else | If there's an answerphone – don't panic! |

Task 9

1. To program the memory on your phone, press MEMORY followed by the key where you want to store the number (0–9)
2. Key in the number you want to store (you can use up to 21 digits).
3. The display shows the number as each key is pressed.
4. Press MEMORY. You hear a beep and the display goes blank to show that the number has been stored in the memory.

Task 12

1. If you are tired, you should go to bed now.
2. You should go to bed now if you are tired.
3. Because you have a busy day tomorrow, you should go to bed now.
4. You should go to bed now because you have a busy day tomorrow.
5. Although you can read until 9:30, you should go to bed now.
6. You should go to bed now, although you can read until 9:30.

F Persuasion exemplars

Task 1   **From paragraph 3:**

Emotive language – chosen to lure you into selecting their services

Why is Broadband better than standard dial up?

1. **It's faster**

Enjoy Internet access up to 10 times faster than a standard 56kbps dial-up connection.

2. **It's always on**

There's no need to wait to get online. You're permanently connected until you turn your PC off.

3. **It keeps your phone line free**

Surf the Internet and talk on the phone at the same time.

4. **It's easy to install**

There is no need to call an engineer. **Once you've registered** we'll send you your broadband modem with simple instructions on how to set this up on your PC.

5. **It's a new experience**

Tiscali Broadband changes the way you use the Internet. **You** can shop and bank online, instantly download music and games in seconds, email large attachments easily, watch music and film clips from your PC, and much more!

new members
join now >>

existing members
upgrade now >>

Headings – to emphasise key messages

Inclusive phrase – chosen to encourage you to want the product

Structure – series of points supporting one viewpoint

Repetition – to drive home key points

Personal pronouns – appealing directly to reader, 'you'

Task 3

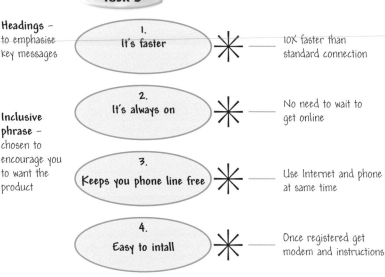

1. **It's faster** — 10X faster than standard connection

2. **It's always on** — No need to wait to get online

3. **Keeps you phone line free** — Use Internet and phone at same time

4. **Easy to intall** — Once registered get modem and instructions

5. **New experience** — Changes way we use Internet

Exemplars

153

Task 5

Association of ideas – wants would-be purchaser to think if they buy this phone they will share some of the glamour of Beckham

Repetitive slogan – emphasises key message

Structure – series of points/images supporting one viewpoint

Inclusive sentence starter – invites reader to join in

practice.

Clever use of language – equating computer games with the professional dedication needed to become a top-class footballer

Personal pronouns – appeals directly to reader with 'you' and 'your'

Brand name and colour – helps the audience recognise company

Task 10

3.
It can be serious

Everything the serious business person needs, e.g. diary, contacts, To Do list, etc.

Email – synchronisation software

4.
It looks great

Good looks are important

Black aluminium finish and small, slim size

Task 11

Refers back to the first paragraph's focus on sound

Sentence signpost – signals additional information about games

> **And it's not just QuickShare™**
>
> It sounds great
> Compose your own 32-bit polyphonic ring tones using the T610's ringtone composer. Plus assign ring tones and sounds to contacts in your address book, along with pictures so you can both see and hear who's calling.
>
> It's great fun
> Superb graphics, excellent sound effects and a joystick control combine to make the T610 the perfect mobile gaming companion. There are extra games available to download via Entertainment on the T610 menu.

Connective – signals additional information about ring tones

Connective – signals additional information about contacts

(G) Argue exemplars

Task 1

From paragraph 4:

Questions directly addressed to reader to guide reader

Topic sentence – introduces focus of paragraph

Sentence signposts – guide the reader

Emotive language – attempt to get audience to agree with argument

> Do you need another reason to hate text messaging? People in education have been warning us, but no one seems to listen. Messaging is killing grammar. Because so many kids use text messages all the time, they've forgotten vowels exist.
>
> The English language is better for the diversity and colloquial terms it has created and the way that it has evolved over the centuries, but such an unnatural form of writing like text messaging will kill all the beauty in the English language. In a world of consumerism, where people are under the impression that they have to rush to do everything, they have decided to cut out verbal communication too. Things have gone too far. Push up the price of texting, push up the price of phones or just burn every single one on the planet. Which is more important; the sanity of a minority or the insanity and illiteracy of the majority. Decide for yourself.

Informal language – suited to web medium

Formal language – makes a serious point but directly addressing reader

Evidence – supports a main point

Series of points – supporting argument

Task 3

4.
Messaging is killing grammar

Kids forget vowels exist

5.
Beauty of English language being killed

Good to have diversity, but gone too far

Everyone rushes everything

Burn all phones or make more expensive

Task 5

Topic sentence – introduces focus of paragraph

Interesting opening – helps hook the reader

Series of points – supports argument

Signals an example

Program Safety

THE Internet **is not a dangerous place**. Millions of people access the Internet every day. <u>**The only reason it seems dangerous is that we only ever hear of it being misused by hackers, paedophiles and other criminals.**</u>

Using programs <u>such as</u> MSN Messenger, <u>users talk only to people who know their email address</u>. Parents should encourage their children to use programs like this and, if they must use less secure programs, to use them safely.

Lecturing and forbidding means only that the child is more likely to want to experience these **<u>forbidden delights</u>**.

(14-year-old boy)

Formal, impersonal, language – uses the third person

Evidence – supports a main point

Emotive language – makes the audience worry about what is happening

---

Task 11

Text jumps to point about more secure programs without making link clear

Again text jumps to a different point without making link clear

Program Safety

THE Internet is not a dangerous place. Millions of people access the Internet every day. **<u>The only reason it seems</u>** dangerous is that we only ever hear of it being misused by hackers, paedophiles and other criminals.

<u>Using programs such as MSN Messenger, users talk only to people who know their email address</u>. Parents should encourage their children to use **programs like this** and, if they must use less secure programs, to use them safely.

<u>Lecturing and **forbidding** means only that the child is more likely to want to experience these **forbidden** delights.</u>

(14-year-old boy)

Sentence signpost links back to opening statement and introduces why people are misled

Refers back to the programs introduced in the topic sentence

Well-constructed sentence – 'forbidden' links the child's response to parents' actions

Conclusion

Each paragraph is well constructed and makes its point clearly. However, the paragraphs are not well linked together so the argument is a bit disjointed.

Task 12

Why the Internet could be seen as dangerous

1. Provides paedophiles with an easy way to contact young people
   Supporting point: Nature of chatrooms
   Paragraph link: At a completely different level...

2. Hackers are determined to create viruses to undermine the system – they might succeed
   Supporting point: Internet provides amazing opportunity for someone to pit their wits against the system
   Paragraph link: Another problem of global importance is...

3. Creates an even bigger gap between the rich and poor in the world
   Supporting point: Access to information is power
   Paragraph link: A final problem, though not so immediately worrying, is...

4. No checks on content of Internet sites, so much of the information may be wrong
   Supporting point: We are used to the fact that information in books has been checked

---

Advice unit exemplars

Task 1

From Section 5:

Series of points in logical order – numbered to strengthen sequence

Clear reasons why advice should be followed

5. **Losing a sense of perspective or becoming fanatical.** However passionately you feel about the issue, <u>try to speak</u> in measured tones and keep your objectivity. That way people will be more inclined to listen and to take notice.

6. **Engaging in internal power struggles and in-fighting.** Remember that you are all on the same side, so don't let your campaign fall apart through in-fighting. <u>Keep your fire power for the real enemy</u>, or you'll end up shooting yourself in the foot.

7. **Letting the morale of your supporters flag.** Whenever <u>you</u> achieve something, however small, let everyone know. It helps maintain interest and <u>gives the impression that the campaign is going somewhere</u>.

Softened form of imperative – makes a suggestion rather than instructing

Conversational, tone – reassures the reader

Throughout, addresses the reader directly as 'you'

Exemplars

Task 3 From Point 5:

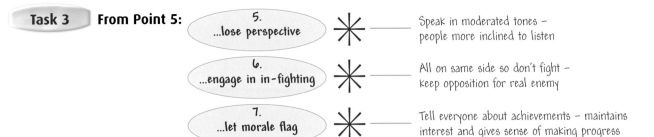

5.
...lose perspective — Speak in moderated tones – people more inclined to listen

6.
...engage in in-fighting — All on same side so don't fight – keep opposition for real enemy

7.
...let morale flag — Tell everyone about achievements – maintains interest and gives sense of making progress

---

Task 7 **Reasons not to smoke**

You can always smell a smoker. No one wants to be smelly but the trouble is, if you smoke, that's exactly what you'll be. And it's no good thinking you can smother the smell with perfume or aftershave.

Task 11 **Six reasons not to smoke**

- makes you smell – no one wants to be smelly – can't cover it up
- it will also cost a fortune – think of all you'll waste on habit – think what else could do with money
- at the same time, suggests you're weak willed – most smokers don't want to smoke, do so because can't give up – no one wants to look weak
- annoys other people – moreover now evidence that passive smoking harmful – consider others
- probably kill you – think how feel in few years if find health problem – do yourself favour & don't start
- will age you quickly

Task 12 Highlighted opening statement is positive but it should be negative to fit in with the list. Therefore it is a misfit and breaks the flow of the text.

4. Whatever you do, do it well. Good presentation need not cost money <u>and it will certainly help you to be taken seriously</u> by others. So adopt a professional attitude at all times.

Task 13 **Six good reasons not to smoke**

Whenever you feel tempted to smoke remember:

1. You can always smell a smoker.
2. You will be wasting your money every time you buy a packet.
3. You may make people think you're weak willed.
4. You may be making your skin wrinkly.
5. You will be annoying many other people.
6. You may very well be killing yourself.

Discursive exemplars

Task 1 **From paragraph 4:**

Formal, impersonal language

Topic sentence – introduces focus of paragraph

Series of paragraphs – present a range of viewpoints

Tentative language – 'could' raises questions

Logical connective – signals change of direction

Signals evidence to follow

Sentence signpost – adds information. Note restrained tone

Present tense

> Moreover, Google can be a worry for organisations as well as governments and individuals. <u>For example,</u> the Church of Scientology is furious that the site listed second in a Google search for "scientology" turns out to be Xenu.net, which is run by a fierce opponent of the cult.[1] Last year the Church's lawyers successfully bullied Google into removing links to Xenu.net and similar sites, until a public outcry forced a climb-down. <u>It could be argued that</u> Google <u>is a threat to individual freedom.</u> <u>But</u> knowing that probably won't make any difference; most of us will carry on using it because <u>it's</u> so good at solving our immediate problems.

Task 3

Conclusion
- Wonderful research aid
- Political phenomenon
- Threat to individual freedom but
- Will use it because solves problems

Task 5

Paragraphs 3 and 4:

Series of paragraphs – presents a range of viewpoints

Sentence signpost – introduces new paragraph. Note restrained tone and use of third person, including the passive

Connective – signals additional point

> Parents who support TV watching <u>argue that it helps</u> them by keeping their children occupied and entertained. <u>They defend allowing children to have their own TVs in the bedroom by saying that this means that children can watch specialist programmes without disturbing the rest of the family,</u> and thus youngsters have more access to educational programmes.
> <u>Moreover, it could be argued</u> that children who are not allowed to watch television are shut out of conversations with friends about what programmes they have seen. The child who is denied access to TV could thus feel very isolated and might, therefore, perform badly at school. <u>In addition,</u> interestingly, some research suggests the ability to understand stories on the television at the age of six is a good predictor of how well children will understand stories when reading them at the age of eight.

Evidence – backs up point

Tentative language – 'could' raises questions

Topic sentence – introduces focus of paragraph

Task 9

Paragraph 1: Questioning the logic

How could anyone argue that Martian communication systems are superior to those on Earth? Let's look at the facts. It has only recently been established that there may well be water on Mars and there is still no evidence of life.

Task 10

Structure B

Introduction: Longstanding debate on whether TV is harmful or not to children

Background: How widespread is TV?

Report found TV is part of life:
- increasingly TV in every bedroom
- not switched off
- parents give way to pressure

Parents 'FOR' TV

✳ Keeps children occupied/entertained

✳ Helps children socialise

✳ Research suggests helps children understand story

TV in bedroom means don't interrupt others and gives access to educational programmes

No TV means shut out of conversations

Parents 'AGAINST' TV

✳ Too much sex and violence

✳ Watch excessive amounts

✳ Undermines creativity — Fail to learn how to play

✳ Stops children interacting — Don't learn social skills

✳ Become couch potatoes — Sit and eat all time

Conclusion:
TV here to stay – unrealistic to oppose, therefore should we limit? — E.g. age limit for TV in bedroom

Introduction to issue				
Signposts/ introducing points **For**			**Signposts/ contrasting points** **Against**	

Signposts/ introducing points

1. The key point that parents who defend television make is

2. A second point in favour

3. An additional point in support

Intro conclusion:

For

1. Entertains children and keeps them happy

2. Helps children learn language because they hear such a range of language

3. Helps children understand the world

Signposts/ contrasting points

1. Parents on the opposite side argue

2. On the other hand, some parents think

3. Other parents strongly disagree, arguing that

Against

1. Makes children very passive

2. Stops children learning language because they just listen and watch and don't speak

3. Exposes young children to things they shouldn't know about

Conclusion summing up issue

Moreover, it **could be argued** that children who are not allowed to watch television are shut out of conversations with friends about what programmes they have seen. The child who is denied access to TV **could** thus **feel very isolated** and **might, therefore, perform badly** at school. In addition, interestingly, some research **suggests** the ability to understand stories on the television at the age of six is a good predictor of how well children will understand stories when reading them at the age of eight.

On the other hand, parents who are worried about the dominance of television **tend to be** concerned not only about programme content but about the mental and physical consequences of endless TV-watching.

They argue that children **could watch** programmes with violent or sexual themes **if they turn on** television after the watershed and that unsupervised youngsters **could watch** excessive amounts of television without parents being aware of it. In addition, they fear that television **might be undermining** children's creativity since time spent watching TV **could be spent** on imaginative play. Thus children **might fail** to learn how to entertain themselves through games and creative play which are an important foundation for learning. Related to this concern is the fear that excessive TV watching **may mean** children fail to learn social skills because they don't interact with other children.

Key point of paragraph

Comment – raises an issue arising from the point

A survey of 1000 13-year-olds reveals that they feel that there should be a recommended age limit for allowing a child to have a television in their bedroom. 62 per cent felt that this age limit should be four. One boy explained: "It's not right is it, leaving a little kid alone with a telly in their bedroom? You just don't know what sort of programmes they might switch on late at night." This raises the question of how should such a recommendation be introduced.

Statistical evidence – backs up point, plus quotation to illustrate it

---

Key point paragraph

Comment – raises an issue arising from the point

The vast majority of students said that the television was on all the time in their homes often as background noise. How widespread this has become is illustrated by the fact that only 10% said that the television in shared areas of the home was often turned off in the evenings..As one girl expressed it: "Sometimes it really irritates me. You're trying to explain something that's really important and mum's not listening because she's trying to find out what's happening on Neighbours. This raises the question of whether it would be a good idea to encourage people to turn the television off when it's just on as background noise.

Statistical evidence – backs up point, plus quotation to illustrate it

Review exemplars

Task 1

From paragraph 3:

Logical structure – begins with introduction, followed by a plot outline and comment

Present tense is the main tense – makes the action seem as if it is happening now

Friendly, informal tone

> The action switches to LA, where John's daughter Stella (Theron) comes on board for an even more daring heist. With a fleet of specially modified Minis, the gang decide to steal the gold for a second time – and not even a spot of downtown traffic will stop them.
>
> Although it takes some time to set up the scam, it doesn't interfere with the rhythm of the film and when those Minis hit the highway it becomes a non-stop action flick. Wahlberg, Theron and Norton are solid enough, but its the comic touches from the support that really stand out – Green as Lyle the techno-nerd, Stratham the getaway man called Handsome Rob and Mos Def, a half-dead explosives expert who's afraid of dogs.
>
> With hardly any swearing, little gratuitous violence and no sex, this is a highly enjoyable romp that the whole family can enjoy. Very va va voom.
>
> **NOW rating ★★★★**
> *A surprisingly successful remake of the British heist classic.*

Wide range of sentence structure – maintains interest

Powerful expanded noun phrases – pack in a lot of information

Task 3

4. Comment — Takes time to set scam up but then non-stop action – comic touches outstanding

5. and 6. Conclusion — Highly enjoyable – family entertainment– four stars

Task 4

Well-constructed sentence – includes noun phrases packing in lots of information

Version 1

> The 1969 original, starring Michael Caine, with its fabulous chase scenes involving nifty Minis speeding around the city of Rome, is something of a cult classic.

Key feature of film – acts as a hook to interest the reader

Lively, informal language – helps engage reader

Present tense – makes it seem as if the action is happening now

Task 6

More formal and direct alternatives	Original informal version
fast Minis	nifty Minis
city-centre traffic congestion	spot of downtown traffic
reach the main road	hit the highway
enjoyable action	enjoyable romp
very thrilling	very va va voom
a fast car driver who enables criminals to leave the crime scene swiftly	getaway man
a person who is obsessed by technical things	techno-nerd

Task 8

From paragraph 3:

Repetition of earlier sentence signpost signals to reader that venue is changing

> The action switches to LA, where John's daughter Stella (Theron) comes on board for an even more daring heist. With a fleet of specially modified Minis, the gang decide to steal the gold for a second time –
>
> and not even a spot of downtown traffic will stop them.
>
> Although it takes some time to set up the scam, it doesn't interfere with the rhythm of the film and when those Minis hit the highway it becomes a non-stop action flick. Wahlberg, Theron and Norton are solid enough, but its the comic touches from the support that really stand out – Green as Lyle the techno-nerd, Stratham the getaway man called Handsome Rob and Mos Def, a half-dead explosives expert who's afraid of dogs.
>
> With hardly any swearing, little gratuitous violence and no sex, this is a highly enjoyable romp that the whole family can enjoy. Very va va voom.
>
> **NOW rating ★★★★**
> *A surprisingly successful remake of the British heist classic.*

Reference to Minis links back to introduction

Connective – emphasises change of direction

Sentence signpost – helps reader recognise key information within sentence

Exemplars

Extract 1

Brackets used to separate names of actors from their roles in the film

The action starts in Venice with an explosive boat chase scene followed by an expertly executed gold robbery by mastermind Charlie (Wahlberg), safe cracker John (Sutherland), and their crew (Edward Norton, Seth Green, Jason Stratham and Mos Def).

Commas only used to separate names in the list

Extract 2

You probably don't know Park and Lloyd by name, but you may know their work: *Wallace & Gromit* (an award-winning series of shorts based on the adventures of a daft inventor and his resourceful dog) or *Creature Comforts* (a truly marvellous, Oscar-winning short featuring interviews with some 'claymation' zoo residents).

Published by HarperCollins*Publishers* Limited
77-85 Fulham Palace Road
Hammersmith
London
W6 8JB

Browse the complete Collins catalogue at:
www.collinseducation.com

© HarperCollins*Publishers* Limited 2004
10 9 8 7 6 5 4 3 2 1
ISBN 0 00 717761 5

Julia Strong and Kim Richardson assert their moral rights to be identified as the authors of this work.

British Library Cataloguing in Publication Data
A Catalogue record for this publication is available from the British Library.

Acknowledgements
The following permissions to reproduce material are gratefully acknowledged:

Text: Extract from *The Wind Singer* © William Nicholson. Published by Egmont Books Ltd. and used with permission, pp9, 10, 11, 148; extract from *Louis Braille* by Beverley Birch, used by permission of Exley Publications Ltd., pp23, 149; extract from *A History of Reading* reprinted by permission of HarperCollins*Publishers* Ltd., © Alberto Manguel, 1996, pp26, 149; the dictionary definitions are reproduced from the *Collins New School Dictionary* with the permission of HarperCollins*Publishers* Ltd., ©HarperCollins*Publishers* Ltd. 2002, pp36, 150; Roberts' design is reproduced by permission of Roberts Radio Ltd., p65, 152; webpage reproduced by permission of Tiscali UK, pp79, 153; advert reproduced by kind permission of Orange Ltd., pp82, 84, 85, 154; advert reproduced by kind permission of Vodafone Ltd., pp82, 84, 85, 87, 154; advert reproduced by kind permission of iTouch UK, pp83, 84, 85; Nike and the Swoosh Design logo are trademarks of Nike Inc. and its affiliates. Used by permission, p83; extract from *The DIY Guide to Public Relations* by Moi Ali © Directory of Social Change 1995, pp109, 156; review of *The Italian Job* first published in *Now* magazine, 24th September 2003, pp136, 159, 160.

Illustrations: Diagram of ear from *Absolute Science 2* by Arnold, Jones, Jones and Poole, 2003, reprinted by permission of Collins Educational Publishers, p53; illustration of running boy by Janek Matysiak, p26.

Whilst every effort has been made both to contact the copyright holders and to give exact credit lines, this has not proved possible in every case.

Project management by Lucy Hobbs
Edited by Nancy Candlin
Cover design by ABA Design Ltd
Cover and internal design by Ken Vail Graphic Design
Printed and bound by Printing Express Ltd., Hong Kong